Henry B. Small

The Canadian handbook and tourist's guide

Giving a description of Canadian lake and river scenery and places of historical interest, with the best spots for fishing and shooting

Henry B. Small

The Canadian handbook and tourist's guide
Giving a description of Canadian lake and river scenery and places of historical interest, with the best spots for fishing and shooting

ISBN/EAN: 9783742876447

Manufactured in Europe, USA, Canada, Australia, Japa

Cover: Foto ©Andreas Hilbeck / pixelio.de

Manufactured and distributed by brebook publishing software (www.brebook.com)

Henry B. Small

The Canadian handbook and tourist's guide

Natural Steps, Montmorenci, near Quebec.

NOTMAN, Photo.

THE
CANADIAN HANDBOOK
AND
TOURIST'S GUIDE.

PRELUDE.

THE NOOKS AND CORNERS OF CANADA, and more especially of the Lower Province, in addition to the interest they awaken as important sources of Commercial and Agricultural wealth, are invested with no ordinary attraction for the Naturalist, the Antiquary, the Historian, and the Tourist in quest of pleasure or of health. We have often wondered why more of the venturesome spirits amongst our transatlantic friends do not tear themselves away, even for a few months, from London fogs, to visit our distant but more favoured clime. How is it that so few, comparatively speaking, come to enjoy the bracing air and bright summer skies of Canada? With what zest could the enterprising or eccentric among them undertake a ramble, with rod and gun in hand, from Niagara to Labrador, over the Laurentian Chain of Mountains, choosing as rallying points, whereat to compare notes, the summit of Cape Eternity in the Saguenay district, and the Peak of Cap Tourmente, or the Cave of the Winds under Niagara Falls. We imagine the atmosphere of those airy positions is as brisk, to say nothing of the diverse incidents of travel and of sport combined, as that in the fiords of Norway, or as the heath-clad peaks of the Dovre-feld afford to so many an English Tourist and Sportsman.

Volumes have been written to make known the inexhaustible mineral, agricultural, industrial, and commercial wealth of this Colony, but few efforts have yet been made to lay before the public, or rather the travelling portion of the public, the natural beauties of its scenery,—its streams, rivers, lakes and forests,—lakes that in beauty, number, and variety of size, no other country in the world can vie with,—replete with fish of every description, within access alike of the million and the millionaire. To the Botanist, during the summer months, perhaps no country offers such varied inducements,—plants flourishing here of almost every class, from the Lichens and Mosses of the Arctic Zone, to the Azalia, Kalmia, and Lady's Slipper of the Sunny South. The very woods are sacred to Flora, and here may be culled specimens of plants within a day's journey of civilization, that 'erst have led the adventurous seeker after Nature's gems to wander for days away from the beaten track, in the far-off prairies of the West, or the tangled swamps and thickets of the South. To the Ornithologist, the Geologist, or the Student of any branch of Natural History, we would say, take a run through the Canadas to increase your collection. Does not almost every British Mail bring out enquiries and orders for the finest specimens of our Fauna and Flora? If weary of naturalizing during the July and

August heats, steam down and take a briny dip at Murray Bay, or Kakouna, or Tadousac. Do you fancy Canadian Highlands?—seek the pleasant shades of Cap à l'Aigle, or Pointe à Pie. Are you inclined for French gaiety and killing toilets?—steer for Kakouna. Do you prefer the *grand monde*, the fashionable place *par excellence?*—then try Tadousac. Each and all of these localities we will endeavour to lay alike before you, with their associations, their scenery, their attractions, and their inducements for the traveller to linger on his journey, and enjoy what he might otherwise pass by, in search of some wider known and less gifted place. Every traveller in Canada from Baron La Hontan, who "preferred the forests of Canada to the Pyrénées of France," to the Hon. A. Murray, Charlevoix, Peter Kalm, Isaac Weld, Heriot, Silliman, Rameau, Augustus Sala, have united in pronouncing the landscape of Lower Canada so majestic, so wild, so captivating withal, as to vie in beauty with the most picturesque portions of the Old or New World; and though we have no ivied ruins dating back to mediæval times, no moated castle or battlemented tower,—though we have no Chatsworths, nor Blenheims, nor Woburn Abbeys, nor Arundel Castles, embellishing the landscape with their architectural beauty,—yet in Lower Canada especially, most of our nooks and corners are hallowed by associations destined to remain ever memorable amongst the inhabitants of its soil.

In the days of yore the Summer Tourist through the Country had no easy means of access to the quiet nooks in the "back country," or the many pleasant resorts our railways have opened out. The old hackneyed journey was as follows :—A few days at Niagara Falls, a hurried trip through the "ambitious little city of the West," Hamilton, a cursory glance at Toronto, a night on Ontario in the close state-room of a steamer, a hurried run through the Lake of the Thousand Islands, a day or two in Montreal and Quebec, omitting more than half the surroundings of the latter city, and the Canadian Tour was considered complete. But now, thanks to the iron horse and its accessories, wild forest-lands, smiling villages beside rivers teeming with the finny tribe, the scenery of Superior and Huron, the Saguenay, the St. Francis, the St. Maurice, all are easy of access—all worthy of a visit, and only awaiting some painter's hand to bring them prominently forward in their beauty. The facilities about to be offered to pleasure-seekers, through the arrangements the celebrated Thomas Cook, of European Tourist fame, has made, to organize excursion parties to and from this country, will doubtless cause hundreds to avail themselves of the opportunity of visiting, at a moderate cost of time and money, this, the hitherto *Ultima Thule* of travel. The trips which have been conducted by him in Europe, have obtained the highest encomiums from all who have participated in them ; and as it is his purpose now to extend them through the United States and Canada, such intercourse will be of real service in opening International courtesies and mutual hospitalities.

We commence with the City of Quebec as being the first place that the Tourist will reach in Summer by Ocean Steamer ; it is the centre of much beautiful and varied scenery, and affording in its vicinity sporting of almost every description.

QUEBEC AND ITS ENVIRONS.

THE CITY OF QUEBEC, excelling in its fortifications any other city on this continent, has justly been styled the Gibraltar of America. From the natural advantages of its position, surmounting the summit of a promontory 350 feet in height, whose ridge extends from Cap Rouge, the western extremity, to Cape Diamond the eastern end, scarcely any more suitable locality could have been found for a fortress. It is washed on the one side by the waters of the St. Lawrence, whose bosom is here freighted with the ships of all nations, and on the other by the placid waters of the St. Charles. Its innumerable and valuable timber coves or berths, extending some miles in length, are crammed with elm, oak, spruce, pine, tamarack, &c., furnishing an export trade of $5,000,000 per annum, and we can at once comprehend why in 1608 Champlain should have selected it as his capital. From the circumstance of quartz crystals, sparkling like diamonds, being found in the dark-coloured slate of which the Cape is composed, it has acquired the name of Diamond. Quebecers ought to be proud of their scenery, and of the "Historical ivy" which clings to the old walls of Stadacona, its original Indian name. In 1629 it was taken by Sir David Kirke, but restored in 1632. In 1690 it was unsuccessfully besieged by Sir Wm. Phipps. It was finally captured by Wolfe in 1759, after a heroic defence by Montcalm. The Americans attacked it in 1775, but they were repulsed, and their General, Montgomery, was slain. Neighbouring cities may grow vast with brick and mortar; their commerce may advance with the stride of a young giant; their citizens may "sit in the high places among the sons of men," but can they ever compare with the fortress of Quebec for historical memories or beautiful scenery ? Looking from the Citadel, having at its feet a forest of masts, the landscape is closed by Cap Tourmente and by the cultivated heights of the *Petite Montagne* of St. Fereol, exhibiting in succession Beauport, L'Ange Gardien, the green slopes of the Island of Orleans, the Heights of Abraham, the Coves with their humming busy noise, St. Michael's Cove especially forming a graceful curve from Wolfe's to *Pointe à Ruisseaux*. Within this area thrilling events once took place, and round these diverse objects historical souvenirs cluster, recalling some of the most important occurrences in North America ; the contest of two powerful nations for the sovereignty of the New World ; an important episode of the revolution, which gave birth to the adjoining Republic. Each square inch of land of these localities, in fact, was measured by the footsteps of some of the most remarkable men in the history of America ; Jacques Cartier, Champlain, Frontenac, Laval, Phipps and Iberville, Wolfe, Montcalm, Arnold, Montgomery, have each at some time or other trod over this expanse. Close by the spot where now stands the English Cathedral, under an elm-tree only recently cut down, tradition states that Champlain first raised his tent. From the Castle of St. Louis in the Citadel, unfortunately destroyed by fire in 1834, Count Frontenac returned to Admiral Phipps that proud answer, as he said, "by the mouth of his cannon," which will always remain recorded in history. On the Plains of Abraham, where Wolfe and Montcalm fell, may be said to have been decided the fate of French dominion in Canada. At the foot of the Citadel stands a tower, where now floats the British flag, where Montgomery and his soldiers all fell, swept by the grape-shot of a single gun manned by a Canadian artilleryman. Again, in Sault-au-Matelot Street, the intrepid Dambourges, sword in hand, drove Arnold and his men from the houses in which they had established themselves.

" History is everywhere around,—she rises from the ramparts replete with daring deeds, and from the plains equally celebrated for feats of arms, and she again exclaims 'here I am.'"

Quebec is divided into the Upper and Lower Town, the ascent from the latter being by a very steep and winding street through Prescott Gate. The site of the Lower Town may be regarded as almost entirely the creation of human industry, having been gained by excavation from the base of the impending precipice, or redeemed from the river by building out into its waters. The wharves are, generally speaking, carried out upwards of 200 yards into the river.

Skirting the bank of the St. Charles, called by Jacques Cartier Port Ste. Croix, a continuation of Lower Town is called St. Rochs, from which, in a circuitous manner, the city ascends to the very border of the Citadel and the Ramparts, the principal access being through Palace Gate. The city is remarkably irregular, and the streets extremely narrow, following the example of all the old French towns ; but, from the massive walls and antiquated appearance of many of its buildings, its appearance is picturesque and romantic. Here and there flights of steps lead the passenger from one street to another, reminding the tourist forcibly of the streets in the islands of Guernsey or of Malta. The fortifications cover an area of forty acres, and beneath them are many spacious and gloomy vaults for the reception of ammunition and stores during a time of war. The tourist, with proper introductions, or if a foreigner, with a note from his Consul, will find no difficulty in obtaining a pass from the military authorities to view them, and will be well rewarded with the sight. The finest prospect that can be enjoyed in the city is obtainable on the ramparts, and though at the signal house a higher altitude can be obtained, yet to lean upon the balustrade of " the platform " in the promenade, just below the Citadel, and gaze *over* the Lower Town, where the hurry of business is going on, and the ships discharging their cargoes, and yet only hear a confused hum,—to see the sailor tugging away, perhaps at the mast-head of his ship, far below you, and yet only hear his loud, clear shout stealing *upward* in the air, is something unique and attractive. Here near this promenade, between the gardens attached to the old Castle of St. Louis, stands an obelisk to the memory of Wolfe and Montcalm.

The religious establishments and buildings are very numerous, ancient, and well endowed; among the most imposing of all is perhaps the Laval University and Seminary, the Cathedral, the Bishop's Palace, and the Church and Convent of St. Ursula. In the Lower Town is a Chapel noticeable on account of its antiquity and the origin of its name—*Notre Dame des Victoires.* It was built and used as a Church before 1690. In that year Sir Wm. Phipps, in attempting to capture Quebec, was defeated, and in consequence the fête of Notre Dame de la Victoire was instituted in this Church for annual celebration. After the shipwreck and destruction of the English fleet under Admiral Walker in 1711 on Egg Island Rocks, which was regarded by the inhabitants not only as a second victory, but as a miraculous interposition in their favour, the present name was imposed on the Church, in order that both events might be commemorated at once. In the growing suburbs of St. John's and St. Rochs, are several handsome and substantial ecclesiastical structures. In 1845 Quebec was visited at an interval of four weeks by two most calamitous fires; but as there is seldom any evil out of which good does not arise, so in this case many old wooden buildings were swept away, which have been replaced by more substantial brick and stone. Amongst the curiosities which will attract the attention of the visitor, is the Golden Dog, "*Le Chien d'Or.*" This is the figure of a dog in a crouching position rudely sculptured *in relievo*, and richly gilded, which stands above the entrance of an ancient house, which was built by

M. Phillibert, a merchant of the city, in the days of Intendant Bigot. It was, a few years ago, the chief entrance to the City Post Office. Connected with it is the following curious story :—M. Phillibert and the Intendant were on bad terms; but under the system then existing, the merchant knew that it was in vain for him to seek redress in the Colony, and determining at some future period to seek redress in France, he contented himself with placing the figure of a sleeping dog in front of his house, with the following lines beneath it, in allusion to his situation with his powerful enemy :

> "Je suis un chien qui ronge l'os,
> En le rongeant je prends mon repos—
> Un jour viendra qui n'est pas venu
> Que je mordrai qui m'aura mordu."

This allegorical language, however, was too plain for Bigot to misunderstand it, and, as the reward of his verse, poor Phillibert received the sword of an officer of the garrison through his back when descending the Lower-Town Hill. The murderer was permitted to leave the Colony unmolested, and was transferred to a regiment in the East Indies, but was pursued thither by a son of the deceased, who, meeting him in the streets of Pondicherry, avenged his father's death.

The environs of Quebec are highly interesting, and we will take a few of the most prominent in turn. *Chateau-Bigot*, some five miles north of Quebec, an antique and massive ruin, standing in solitary loneliness in the centre of a clearing, at the foot of the Charlesbourg mountain, is well worthy of a visit. Those who wish to go there, are strongly advised to take the cart-road which leads from Charlesbourg Church, turning up near the house of a man named Charles Paquet. Pedestrians will prefer the other route; they can, in this case, leave their vehicle at Mrs. Huot's boarding-house, a little higher than the Church, and then walk through the fields, skirting during the greater part of the road a beautiful brook. But by all means let them take a guide with them. A tragical occurrence enshrines the old building with a tinge of mystery, which only awaits the pen of a novelist to weave out of it a thrilling romance. The legend may be condensed as follows:—Somewhere about the year 1757, the French Intendant, Bigot, who had charge of the public funds of Canada, attempted to lead here the same dissolute life which the old Noblesse of France led before the French Revolution, and built this country seat in which to seek relaxation from the cares of office. Hunting was a favourite pastime of this old noble, and this indefatigable Nimrod on one occasion, tracking a deer which he had wounded, strayed far away from his chateau, and was overtaken by the shades of evening in the midst of a dense forest. Exhausted with hunger and fatigue, he sat down to ponder on what course he should pursue, when, startled by the sound of footsteps, he perceived before him a light figure, with eyes as black as night, and raven tresses flowing in the night wind. It was an Algonquin beauty, one of those ideal types whose white skin betray their hybrid origin—a mixture of European blood with that of the Aboriginal race. It was Caroline, a child of love, born on the banks of the Ottawa, a French officer her sire, and the Algonquin tribe of the Beaver claimed her mother. Struck with the sight of such beauty, he requested her guidance to his castle, as she must be familiar with every path of the forest. . . . The Intendant was a married man, but his lady seldom accompanied her lord on his hunting excursions, remaining in the Capital; but it was soon whispered abroad, and came to her ears, that something more than the pursuit of wild animals attracted him to his country seat. Jealousy is a watchful sentinel, and after making several visits to the castle, she verified her worst fears. . . . On the night of the 2nd July, when every inmate was wrapped in slumber, a masked person rushed upon this "fair Rosamond," and plunged a dagger to the hilt in her heart. The whole household was alarmed; search was made, but no clue to the murderer discovered. A variety of reports were circulated, some tracing the deed to the late Intendant's wife, others alleging that the avenging mother of the *métisse* was the assassin. A mystery, however, to this day surrounds the deed. She was buried in the cellar of the castle, and the letter C engraved on a flat stone, which, till within the last few years, marked her resting-place. The chateau at once fell into disuse and decay; and a dreary solitude now surrounds the dwelling and the tomb of that dark-haired child of the wilderness, over which green moss and rank weeds cluster profusely. Such is the legend of Chateau-Bigot.

The Hotels in Quebec, of which the St. Louis and Russell's are the principal, are very good, and moderate in their terms; carriages are easily procured anywhere, and street cars have lately been introduced into the city. The principal buildings are the Custom House, the Marine Hospital, the Parliament Buildings, and the different gates, which were formerly the only entrances to the city. To SPENCER WOOD, the residence of the Governor-General, is a very pleasant drive, and the view thence is magnificent.

THE STE. FOY MONUMENT stands in an open field, on the brow of a cliff, from which the view is beautiful in the extreme, and is reached after a five or six minutes' walk from the Ste. Foy Toll-gate, through an avenue bordered on either side by handsome villas, and fine gardens, and half-shaded by over-arching trees. As you turn towards the monumental pillar, you have before you the valley of the St. Charles, along which the populous suburbs of St. Roch and St. Sauveur are gradually making their way. Beyond the limit of the level ground, the hills rise up terrace-like, bright with verdure, and rendered still more attractive by the endless succession of villas, farm houses, and villages, which dot the rising ground at intervals, until they are lost in the distance, far away behind Lorette and Beauport, where the blue summits of the Laurentian range rise to the skies. The monument is decidedly the handsomest public monument in or near the city. Of bronzed metal, standing on a stone base, and surmounted by a bronze statue of Bellona, it is a most prominent object in the landscape. The face of the pedestal fronting the Ste. Foy road has the simple inscription, surrounded by a laurel wreath, "Aux Braves de 1760, érigé par la Société St. Jean Baptiste de Québec, 1860." On the face looking towards the city is the name "Murray," on an oval shield surmounted by the arms of Great Britain and Ireland, and supported by British insignia. On the other side is a shield bearing the name "Levis," surmounted by the arms of France under the Bourbons, the crown and the lilies, with appropriate supporters. In rear, looking towards the valley, there is a representation of a wind-mill in bas-relief—in allusion, we suppose, to the wind-mill which was an object of alternate attack and defence to both armies on the occasion of the battle. This portion of the column also bears the national arms of Canada.—The idea of erecting a monument here was conceived many years ago. For a long time the plough of the farmer and the shovel and pick-axe of the workman, as he labored at the foundation of new buildings along the Ste. Foy road, turned up human remains— evidently the relics of the slain. Rusty, half-decayed arms, accoutrements and buttons, bearing the arms of the French and British regiments, told to whom they belonged. In 1853-'4 an unusual number of these bleached fragments of humanity were found, and the St. Jean Baptiste Society conceived the idea of having them all interred in one spot. They were accordingly collected, and the Christian intention of the Society was carried out on the 5th June 1854, when the national societies, troops, volunteers, public bodies, &c., followed in procession a magnificent funeral car containing the bones of the slain to this their last resting place.—The battle of Ste. Foy was one of no ordinary character, being the first and only action which was fought in the course of the De Levis' bold attempt to wrest the Fortress City from the British, and was also the last victory won by French arms on Canadian soil. Quebec, during that winter, was held by but a handful of British troops, and the occasion seemed most auspicious for the French. The battle lasted one hour and three-quarters, and from accurate data about 4000 corpses strewed the environs of the spot where the monument now stands.

Stretching southwards, the next object of historical interest is the expanse of table land known as THE PLAINS OF ABRAHAM, celebrated in history as being the death scene of Wolfe and Montcalm. The battle ground presents almost a level surface from the brink of the St. Lawrence to the Ste. Foy Road. The Grande Allée, or Road to Cap Rouge, running parallel to that of Ste. Foy, passes through its centre. On the highest ground, considerably in advance of the Martello Towers, not far from the fence which divides the race-ground from the enclosures on the east, are the remains of a redoubt, close by which, a rock is pointed out as marking the spot where Wolfe actually breathed his last, and in one of the enclosures near to the road is the well whence they brought him water. Montcalm, who survived some twelve hours, was buried in an excavation made by the bursting of a shell within the precincts of the Ursuline Convent,—a fit resting place for the remains of a man who died fighting for the honor and defence of his country; but England, jealous of the ashes of Wolfe, laid them beside his father's at Greenwich, the town in which he was born. The skull of Montcalm was exhumed some ten or twelve years ago, and placed in a glass case in the Convent, where the curious in relics can see it on application to the chaplain there. The monument in Quebec, common to Wolfe and Montcalm,—the stone placed in the Ursuline Convent in honor of the latter,—and the smaller column, on the plains dyed with the blood of

Wolfe, form a complete series of testimonials, honorable to the spirit of the age, and the distinguished individuals under whose auspices they have been erected. The memorial on the Plains bears the following inscription: "Here died Wolfe; victorious; 1759."

A ride to THE FALLS OF MONTMORENCI, seven miles down the river, will abundantly repay the tourist for any trouble or expense to which he may be subjected. The Montmorenci itself, so called after a French Admiral of that name, is an inconsiderable stream,—but having made a leap of two hundred and fifty feet, is quite deserving of its reputation. The sheet of water comes over the precipice in an unbroken mass, discharging its translucent treasure into a pool below, which boils and foams as if venting its wrath at having been tossed about, till in a few moments it glides onward in peace, to mingle with the current of the St. Lawrence. The narrowness of the fall, being only 50 feet in width, when compared with its height, perhaps, causes the latter to seem greater than it really is. The whole of the scenery on the road through Beauport and back again by an interior road is full of interest. About two miles above the fall is a curious formation on the river bank called The Natural Steps; these are a series of layers of the limestone rock, each about a foot in thickness, forming the river bank, and, for about half a mile, receding one above the other to the height of about 20 feet as regularly as if framed by the hand of man. They are an object of curiosity, and being so near the fall, should be included in the visit. Facing the roaring cataract stands the "Mansion House," the summer residence of an English Prince, the Duke of Kent, in 1791. The main portion of the "Mansion House," is just as he left it; the room in which he used to write is yet shown; a table and chair, part of his furniture, are to this day religiously preserved, and access can be had to view the place through the kindness of the proprietor, G. B. Hall, Esquire, whose

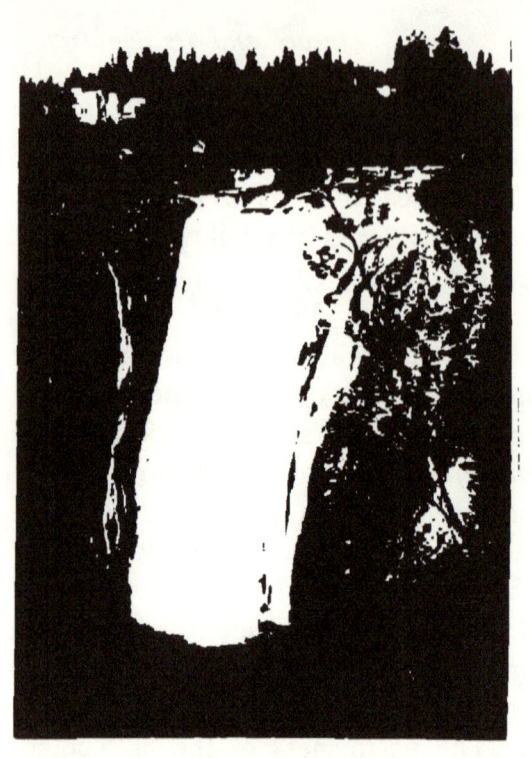

Montmorenci Falls, near Quebec.

NOTMAN. Photo.

saw-mills lie just below the falls. Montmorenci Falls in winter are a favorite resort for the residents of Quebec, who drive there, warmly wrapped up in buffalo robes, in their light carioles or sleighs; and carrying with them a basket well stocked, enjoy what is unknown elsewhere in midwinter, a picnic on the snow. The foam and spray rising from the foot of the falls accumulate in the shape of ice, forming a cone sometimes nearly 100 feet high. A second one of less size is also formed, which is greatly (the higher cone, only by the more hardy and venturesome) made use of by visitors for "coasting" and "toboggining;" that is, having ascended to the summit, they entrust themselves to their small sleigh or toboggin, as the case may be, and slide down at full speed, gaining a velocity every instant, which carries them sometimes half a mile or more on the surrounding level ice. It requires, however, the expertness of boys used to "coasting" to steer straight down the incline, and it not unfrequently happens that two or three upsets, though generally without any serious consequences, take place. The cold is not felt by those engaged in the sport, so thoroughly does the exercise warm the blood. We do not know of any exercise more invigorating than guiding a toboggin at full speed down an incline of 45° when two or three ladies are clinging on behind, and we recommend all who have never enjoyed this sport, to try their hands, if only for once, at this entirely Canadian amusement. A toboggin is a light Indian sleigh made of very thin wood and curled over in front, and used chiefly by pleasure parties in sliding down hill sides covered with crusted but lightly packed snow—small sleighs with runners are chiefly used at the ice cones. From the summit of the large ice-cone, the glassy sides slope down evenly in all directions; one, leading down swift into the huge boiling caldron at the foot of the cascade, the other, the side up which we climb. A few years ago the soldiers of the garrison held a picnic here in winter, when the cone was excavated into a grotto and alcoves, which, when illuminated at night, presented a most beautiful sight, conveying an idea of the winter palace of St. Petersburg on the Neva.—To those who have not resided in Quebec during the winter, it is hardly possible to convey an idea of the interest which is felt in the formation of an "ice-bridge." When the ice does not take between the two shores, there is often much difficulty in crossing the river. The stream is then full of masses of floating ice, varying in size from a few feet square to many hundred feet, through and over which the traveller is taken in a canoe. Should the boatmen be fortunate enough to strike a good crossing, and get clear water, the journey is quickly made, and is not unpleasant. This, however, is not always the case, and sometimes the victim of circumstances is carried about for hours on the ice, and landed at last some miles from the place he set out for. Despite the apparent danger of the traverse, we very rarely hear of a canoe being lost, and we have never heard of any fatality resulting from an accident. The "ice-bridge" generally holds till the latter end of April, and breaks up all at once.

As pleasant a drive as the stranger can have in the environs of Quebec is, taking the Cap Rouge Road, out by St. Lewis Gate, and returning by the Ste. Foy Road, nine miles or more. This drive takes us through SILLERY, a place of great historical interest. Here De Maisonneuve passed his first winter with the colonists intended to found Montreal. A chapel, missionary residence, hospital, fort, and houses, were all substantially built in this spot, and twenty years ago Abbé Ferland saw a portion of the church walls standing. At the centre of Sillery Cove is a cape, not very high, but with its sides perpendicular. This was the fort; on the left is the missionary's house, now converted into a residence for the clerks of H. LeMesurier, Esq. The building has been kept in repair, and is still in a good state of preservation. In a line with it, can be discovered the foundation of the church. In this neighbourhood is situated MOUNT HERMON CEMETERY; it lies on the south side of the St. Lewis Road, and slopes irregularly, but beautifully, down the cliff overhanging the St. Lawrence. It was laid out by Major Douglas, the engineer who designed Greenwood Cemetery, New York. A drive, upwards of two miles in extent, affords access to all parts of the grounds. Many beautiful monuments adorn them, and in the front stands the handsome temple called St. Michael's Chapel, which is weekly attended by the Sovereign's representative and suite, and rank and fashion of the city. Leaving this spot, the ride continues through the woods on the edge of the banks rising from the shore. On the south side are distinguished the embouchures of the Etchemin and Chaudière pouring in their tribute of waters. The view from Pointe à Ruisseaux is worthy the attention of any artist. A little further on are the ruins of what was once a large stone chapel. A visit to the Church of Ste. Foy, from which is seen, below, the St. Charles, gliding smoothly through its valley, with the villages of Lorette and Charlesbourg in the distance, must not be omitted.

The other Cemeteries worthy of a visit are Belmont, on the Ste. Foy Road, and St. Charles on Little River Road, each about three miles from the city.

The Indian village of Lorette is nine miles, Lake St. Charles twelve miles, and Lake Beauport eighteen miles from Quebec. Each repays the visitor in beauty. But by all means make a downward voyage from Lake St. Charles to the Lorette Falls in a birch canoe, for the sake of getting even but a glimpse of CASTORVILLE, a forest-wild, through which the St. Charles, mantled over by a dense growth of spruce and fir trees, intersected by a maze of avenues, glides, having passed through a distance of eight miles of perfectly fairy navigation. The mansion lies on a point formed by the Grand Désert and St. Charles streams: along the banks are little bowers of birch-bark, and boats and canoes anchored around, close by a veritable wigwam. This is the home of the Hon. L. Panet, whom the Lorette Huron Indians have elected as their honorary chief.

There is a remarkable echo at Lake St. Charles, which, unlike other echoes, tarries some few seconds before repeating the sound uttered ; and this in its turn is re-echoed from another quarter, as though the nymph of the Lake were summoning the dryads of the neighbouring woods to join in the sport.

THE LOWER ST. LAWRENCE.

Thirty-six miles below Quebec lies a small group of islands, of which the largest—CRANE ISLAND—is only six, and GOOSE ISLAND four and a half miles in length. They are united by a belt of low land, covered with most luxuriant hay, and are the resort of myriads of geese, ducks and teal ; and not only in the fall and spring do they congregate there, but they make it also their breeding place. The high tides of spring and fall wash the foot of the rising ground on which the manor house of these islands stands, and at such times the game, such as ring-plovers, curlews, sea-snipe, sand-pipers, &c., alight within a few rods of the house. To the north of Crane Island lies a smaller one, which the tide covers daily ; that is the *Dune*, well known to Canadian *Chasseurs* as abounding with Canadian geese, (*outardes,*) snow-geese and ducks. "Every day in May and September," says Le Moine, "you may see a flock of snow-geese and *outardes* feeding there, some three thousand in number, beyond a rifle's range, or winging their rapid, noisy, wedge-like flight towards the muddy St. Joachim flats opposite." On the long sand-bar known as *Batture aux Corneilles*, you may at times see a dense vapor, to all appearance, hovering over it, that you might take for a squall of rain or hail, but soon the snowy breasts of myriads of chubby little northern strangers, the ring-plovers, are to be seen settling on the sand; now is your time,—enfilade their ranks; fire low—one shot suffices; to fire again, would only cause unnecessary carnage. The Seigneury of these islands belongs to the McPherson family, who, to their praise be it said, are indefatigable in enforcing the game laws and punishing trespassers; but their permission is easily obtained for a day's shooting, by a true sportsman. Within the last five years, two guns in two days killed fifty wild geese there. Crane Island has its legend attached to it. More than a century ago a French officer left Old for New France, as Canada was then called. He obtained the grant of a Seigneury comprising a group of islands called the Ste. Marguerite, including Goose and Crane Islands, and thereon he built, not a baronial castle, not a crenelated tower, but a plain, massive, stone house—a prison, as it proved subsequently, for himself—or for his son; tradition has failed to elucidate the point. There for many a long year a solitary prisoner was immured. His keeper, perhaps his friend, his relative—was a woman of rank and wealth. The prisoner, it was said, was insane. The question was often asked, Were there no lunatic asylums in France fit to receive him? Dark surmises were circulated. Who was this new Masque de Fer? Why was he thus immured? The name of the fair occupant of the manor was Madame de Granville; the prisoner was . . . her brother—sisterly love made her his jailor—she said so. Years rolled on, the captive died, and though till recently the ruins of the grim old house were standing, on its site a modern structure has been erected. It required great effort to disjoint the masonry of the old walls.

Steaming down the North Channel after passing Château

Richer, the pretty little Church of Ste. Anne, nestling under the brow of a steep hill, forms one of the most attractive features of the landscape. Hither annually repair the blind, the lame and the halt, to invoke the interposition of the Saint to make them whole. A number of crutches left behind by persons cured, were formerly hung up in the church, but within late years they have been removed to the sacristy. The inside walls are adorned with strange paintings, of a primitive nature, with singular explanations difficult to be understood. The environs are very pleasing; the neat white cottages ever and anon peering out from a dense covert of evergreens, maple or birch. Many places of no little interest abound in the neighbourhood, such as the Falls of Ste. Anne, the Féréol Falls, and the Seven Falls. In fact, there is scarcely to be found in the world a bolder or finer ravine than that through which the Ste. Anne finds its way down from the mountains to the St. Lawrence. It is as well or better worth seeing than Niagara, without its *renommée*. From the top of the hill overhanging the village, the view is extensive, taking in the whole northern shore of the Island of Orleans, with Grosse Isle, (the Quarantine Station,) looming up in the distance.

The Château Richer swamps, in spite of the indiscriminate slaughter of birds, still furnish some 3,000 or 4,000 snipe per season. The Bijou marsh, under the Ste. Foy heights, formerly an excellent hunting ground, still furnishes snipe enough to make a good day's sport; but only in certain states of the weather can it be relied on: when a north-east or east wind blows heavily, birds may be met with abundantly. Woodcock are numerous at Côte-à-Bonhomme, near Charlesbourg, at La Baie du Febvre, Les Salines, and in almost any part of the thick cedar swamps which lie over five miles away from the city. Large game in the vicinity is scarce. A curious incident, however, recently occurred to a sporting member of the Quebec bar, whom the summer vacation had seduced away from his Blackstone and Coke, to the swampy Chateau Richer flats. He was bagging a few birds leisurely, when on firing his first shot, he heard a rustling in the bushes, and out stepped—a bear. Sympathy for a fellow-sportsman ought to have saved Bruin's life; not so, however; his presence on the swamp was construed by the disciple of St. Hubert into a clear case of trespass. A heavy charge at close quarters, and Bruin was no more.

The shores of the whole of the Lower St. Lawrence are probably unequalled in the world for the numbers and variety of wild-fowl which frequent them. In the fall of the year especially, they literally swarm with ducks, teal, and other sea-fowl. September brings forth from their breeding places in the barren wilds of Labrador, and secluded lakes and islands of the North, myriads of sand-pipers, curlew, plover, &c. At the entrance of the Gulf, the Bird Rocks are tenanted by large numbers of gannets, puffins, guillemots, auks and kittiwakes, and their eggs are an article of traffic to some of the neighbouring coasters, Capt. Fortin, four years ago, having come upon several schooners loading up with eggs at these islands. Here the egg collector may supply his collection with many rare specimens. The largest of them, or, as it is also called, Gannet Rock, is the easiest of access, the southerly side being the only place where a boat can land. But the ascent cannot be made from here; the only spot whence that can be accomplished is from a rocky point on the north-west, and then it is very difficult, as it is necessary to jump from a boat, thrown about by the surf, on to the inclined surface of a ledge, rendered slippery by the fuci that cover it. The landing once accomplished, the first ascent is easy, but the upper part both difficult and dangerous, as the rock is so soft it cannot be trusted to, and, in addition, rendered slippery from the constant trickling from above, and the excrements of the birds that cover it in all directions. We have ourselves seen thousands of water-fowl gobbling up the shell-fish, barnacles, &c., which cling to the shelving rocks round Plateau and Bonaventure Islands at Gaspé. We have watched the gannet, the herring-gull, the cormorant, hovering in clouds over Percé Rock, on whose verdant summit they build and find an asylum secure from their great destroyer—man. We have seen their young shot by thousands for food in the month of August. It is not an uncommon thing in the fall of the year for the Gaspé fishermen to kill as many as twenty ducks at one shot in the air-holes among the ice, down which the hungry birds crowd to feed.

Where is the Canadian sportsman who would not give almost the world for a week on the Mille Vaches shoals in September? Where is the fowler who has not heard of the sport which Jupiter River, on Anticosti, affords?

Father Point, lower down than Rimouski, during strong easterly winds, affords capital sport; Canada geese, Brent geese and ducks, are perpetually hovering over the extreme end of the point; the fowler, carefully concealed, pours a deadly volley into the flock, and his faithful Newfoundland dog springs into the surf and fetches out the dead birds.

The Perroquet Rocks, at the entrance of the Straits of Belle Isle, which have acquired an unenviable notoriety by the loss of the North Briton, abound in puffins or sea-parrots, pretty little web-footed birds about the size of pigeons, and marked with variegated colours,—hard to kill and tough to eat.

Six miles further down the coast is the Hudson Bay Company's Post, at the mouth of the celebrated salmon river Mingan. The resident agent there was a leader of one of the exploring parties for Sir John Franklin. Any sportsman whose ardour leads him to these sequestered haunts, will find in Mr. J. Anderson a most hearty friend.

Seal Rocks, in the Traverse, a broad reach in the river, about 18 miles in length, are a delightful small game preserve, so bountifully stocked with ducks, teal, and plover, that a club of chasseurs of St. Jean Port-Joli have leased it from government; a rare thing in Canada, for natives to pay for the privilege of shooting game.

Grouse shooting also affords amusement on the wooded slopes of the hills; but go into the interior about forty miles, in September, and the *whirring* of the grouse from every covert will amply repay your toil; perhaps too you may be lucky enough to have a shot at the king of birds, the golden eagle or his pilfering compeer the bald eagle, soaring high above your head among the crags. And if perchance camped for the night in a deserted sugar-hut, you hear the horrible hooting of the great horned owl, fear nothing; wait until the nocturnal marauder lights on the large tree near your resting place, and by the light of the moon you will soon add to your museum, one of the noblest and fiercest birds of the Canadian fauna.

That portion of the St. Lawrence extending between Goose Island and the Saguenay River, is about twenty miles wide. The spring tides rise and fall a distance of eighteen feet; the water is salt, but clear and cold, and the channel very deep. Here may be seen abundantly the black seal, the white porpoise, and the black whale. The white porpoise yields an oil of the best quality, and the skin is capable of being tanned into durable leather. It is far from being a shy fish, and when seen in large numbers, presents a beautiful and unique appearance. There are two methods used for capturing it, the first of which affords most exciting sport. A boat is used with a white bottom, behind which the fisherman tows a small wooden porpoise, painted of a dark slate color, in imitation of the young of this species. With these lures the porpoise is brought into the immediate vicinity of the harpoon, which is then thrown with fatal precision. The other method is by fencing them in. This fish is fond of wandering over the sand bars at high water, for the purpose of feeding. The fishermen enclose one of these sandy reefs with poles set about fifty feet apart, and a net stretched across. They leave an appropriate opening for the porpoises, which enter at high water, and owing to their timidity, are kept confined by the slender barrier until the tide ebbs, when they are destroyed in great numbers with very little trouble.

—When in Quebec the tourist should by all means take a run down to the Saguenay. This he can do by taking the railway at Pointe Lévi for Rivière du Loup, and there crossing by steamer; or during the summer months he can take steamer to the Saguenay, from Quebec. How is it, many are led to inquire, that so little has been known of the Saguenay and its surroundings, until quite recently? Two reasons may be assigned for this; it is a portion of that vast territory which has been under the jurisdiction of the Hudson Bay Company,—and the wilderness through which it runs is of such a character that its shores can never be greatly changed in appearance. Only a small proportion of its soil can ever be brought under cultivation, and as its forests are a good deal stunted, its lumbering resources are by no means inexhaustible. The wealth it contains is mineral, of which iron is abundant; and that it would yield an abundance of fine marble, the observant eye can judge for itself, as it will frequently fall upon a broad vein of that rock as pure as alabaster. The Saguenay is the largest tributary of the great St. Lawrence, and unquestionably one of the most remarkable rivers on the continent. It is the principal outlet of Lake St. John, which is its head-water; a lake about forty miles long, surrounded with a heavily timbered and rather level country; its waters are remarkably clear, and abound in a great variety of uncommonly fine fish. Eleven large rivers fall into it, yet it has only this one outlet. Into this lake there is a noteworthy Curtain Fall of two hundred and thirty-six feet, so conspicuous as to be seen at forty or fifty miles distant —the Indian name of which is " Oueat Chouan," or " Do you

Calm on the Saguenay.

NOTMAN, Photo.

see a fall there?" The climate in the vicinity of the lake is said to be preferable to that of the sea coast. The lake lies about 150 miles north-east of the St. Lawrence and nearly due north of Quebec. The original Indian name of the Saguenay was Chicoutimi, signifying deep water; but the early Jesuit missionaries gave it the name it now bears, said to be a corruption of St. Jean Nez. The scenery here is wild and romantic in the highest degree. The first half of its course averages half a mile in width, and runs through an untrodden wilderness; it abounds in falls and rapids, and is only navigable for the Indian canoe. A few miles below the southern fall on the river is the village of Chicoutimi, at the junction of a river of the same name, which is the outlet of a long lake named Kenocami, with the Saguenay. Here is a range of rapids which extends ten miles. The Indians say there is a subterranean fall above the foot of the rapids which they call "Manitou," or the "Great Spirit." To avoid these falls there is a carrying place called "Le Grand Portage." An extensive lumber business is transacted here; the village has an ancient appearance, and contains about five hundred inhabitants. The only curiosity is a rude Catholic Church, said to have been one of the earliest founded by the Jesuits. It occupies the centre of a grassy lawn, surrounded with shrubbery, backed by a cluster of wood-crowned hills, and commands a fine prospect, not only of the Saguenay, but also of the spacious bay, formed by the confluence of the two rivers. In the belfry of this venerable church hangs a clear-toned bell, with an inscription upon it which has never yet been translated or expounded. From ten to twelve miles south of Chicoutimi, there recedes from the Saguenay, to the distance of several miles, a beautiful expanse of water called GRAND, or HA! HA! BAY. The village of Grand Bay, 132 miles from Quebec, is the resort of those who want to remain any time here. The name Ha! Ha! is said to be derived from the surprise which the French experienced when they first entered it, supposing it still the river, until their shallop grounded on the north-western shore. At the northern head of it is another settlement called Bagotville. Between these two places the Saguenay is rather shallow, (when compared with the remainder of its course,) and varies in width from two and a half to three miles. The tide is observable as far north as Chicoutimi, and this entire section of the river is navigable for ships of the largest class, whose legitimate home is the ocean, but which ascend thus far for lumber.

That portion of the Saguenay extending from Ha! Ha! Bay to the St. Lawrence, a distance of from fifty to sixty miles, is greatly distinguished for its wild and picturesque scenery. The shores are composed principally of granite, and every bend presents to view an imposing bluff, the majority of which are from eight to fifteen hundred feet high. And generally speaking these towering bulwarks are not content to loom perpendicularly into the air, but they must needs bend over, as if to look at their own features reflected in the water below. Awful beyond expression is it in sailing along the Saguenay, to raise the eyes heavenward, and behold, hanging directly overhead, a mass of granite apparently ready to totter and fall, and weighing perhaps a million tons. Nowhere else have we ever experienced such a sense of human littleness, unless it be at the base of Table Rock at Niagara. Descending from Ha! Ha! Bay, a perpendicular rock, nine hundred feet high, is the abrupt termination of a lofty plateau called THE TABLEAU, a column of dark-coloured granite, 600 feet high by 300 wide, its sides as smooth as if they had just received the polishing stroke from the artisan's chisel. STATUE POINT is another gem of scenery; but what pen can describe the stupendous promonotories, TRINITY POINT and CAPE ETERNITY? The water is as deep five feet from their base, as it is in the centre of the stream, and from actual measurement, many portions of it have been ascertained to be a thousand feet, and the shallowest parts not less than a hundred ; and from the overhanging cliffs, it assumes a black and ink-like appearance. Cape Eternity is the most imposing, and with it is associated the following :—An Indian hunter having followed a moose to the brow of the cliff, after the deer had made a fatal spring far down into the deep water, lost his foothold and perished with his prey. Two or three years ago two fine specimens of the bird of Washington, that rare eagle, were shot here, according to Le Moine, in his *Oiseaux du Canada;* and ever and anon the flight of the bald-headed eagle along the summits of these beetling cliffs,—the salmon leaping after its insect prey,—or the seals bobbing their heads out of the water,—continually attract the sportsman's eye. The village of ST. JEAN, or St. Johns, is a small lumbering village, similar to the few other settlements in this section, and possessing no peculiar attraction except the bay on which it stands, and which appears perhaps more beautiful than it really is, from contrast with the bold shores encircling it. Nearing the St. Lawrence we pass two hills called the PROFILES, from their strong resemblance to human features, and Tête de Boule, a remarkable, round mountain, as stupendous as Capes Trinity or Eternity, meets the view. The current of the Saguenay flows in some places at the rate of seven miles an hour, but when there is any wind at all, it generally blows quite heavily from the north or south. To the European tourist, the appearance of the whole of this river must strongly remind him of the *fiords* of Norway, only on a gigantic scale. For the benefit of summer tourists we would mention the fact that during the "season," or about two months in summer, a steamer from Quebec makes weekly trips, by way of Rivière du Loup, to the Saguenay.

TADOUSSAC, which of late years has come into notice as a place of summer resort, 140 miles below Quebec, lies a little above Pointe aux Vaches, at the east entrance of the Saguenay, about five miles from its confluence with the St. Lawrence, and is situated on a semi-circular terrace at the top of a beautiful bay with a sandy beach, hemmed in by mountains of solid rock, thus presenting a secure retreat from almost every wind. Tadoussac, apart from its pleasant situation as a watering place, is interesting from the circumstance of its having been at an early period the capital of the French settlements, and for a long time was one of the chief fur-trading posts. Here are the ruins of a Jesuit religious establishment, which are considered the great curiosity of this region. Their appearance is not imposing, as you can discover nothing but the foundations upon which the ancient edifice rested; but it is confidently asserted that upon this spot once stood the first stone and mortar building ever erected on the Continent of America—the home of Father Marquette, who subsequently explored the waters of the Mississippi. From the very centre of the ruin has grown up a cluster of pine trees, which must have existed at least two hundred years. The fate, and the very names of those who first pitched their tents in this wilderness, and here erected an altar to the God of their fathers, are alike unknown. Charlevoix, in 1720, thus speaks of it: "Most of our geographers have placed a town here, where there never was but one French house and some huts of savages, who resorted hither annually to trade with the French when the navigation was free; the missionaries made use of the opportunity, and when the trade was over, the merchants returned to their homes, the savages to their forests, and the Gospel labourers followed the last."

Although the salmon is met with in all the streams below Quebec, it is most abundant on the north shore of the St. Lawrence, and in those waters which are beyond the jurisdiction of civilization. It usually makes its appearance about the 20th May, and continues in season for two months. It is an important article of export from this region, and together with trout, affords excellent sport to the visitor at Tadoussac. The Ste. Marguerite, which is one of the chief tributaries of the Saguenay, and can be reached in a boat after a few hours' pull from Tadoussac, abounds with fish, and if the tourist desires remaining on its banks for a few days, he can get accommodation (rough but clean), at the little hamlet of Ste. Marguerite. Another river which affords good fishing in this region is the Esquemain, which empties into the St. Lawrence about twenty miles east of the Saguenay. It is a cold, clear, and rapid stream, abounding in rapids and deep pools, and although there is a saw mill at its mouth, (the enemy of the salmon,) yet its water-works are so arranged as not to interfere with the running of the salmon. The best spot here is at the foot of the fall, which forms a sheet of foam, about one mile above its mouth. Up the stream, owing to its bushy shores, you must fish standing on boulders in the water, and after hooking a fish plunge into the current, which is not deep, and trust to fortune. But the sport these waters afford is more than counterbalanced by the black fly and musquito which swarm here. To ward off their attacks, we would recommend the fisherman to hang a gauze veil over his neck and face, or carry with him some oil of rosemary, which is a sure preventive to the bites of these merciless marauders. The mouth of the Saguenay itself is hemmed in with barriers of solid rock, and when the tide is flowing in, first-rate sport may be obtained from one of these points; but we must warn the stranger to be carefully on his guard, lest, engrossed with his rod and fly, the incoming tide, which rises very suddenly, surrounds the rock on which he stands, and he be necessitated to swim through the cold and turbulent current till he reach the main shore. Next to the salmon, the finest game fish here are trout, which are taken in both the fresh and salt water, and possess a flavor which the fish of the western rivers and lakes do not possess. They run from two to fifteen pounds in weight in the Lower St. Lawrence and all its tributaries. Those of the Saguenay, however, are the largest, most abundant, and of the finest quality. Almost every bay or cove is crowded with trout, and, generally speaking, the rocks upon which you have to stand afford an abundance of room to swing and drop the fly. Besides this, fishing in this region possesses a charm which the angler seldom experiences elsewhere, viz.: the uncertainty as to the character of the prize before it is landed, as it may be a common, or salmon-trout, or a regular-built salmon. It is reported of a celebrated Quebec sportsman, that he captured in one week on the Esquemain seventy salmon, and upwards of a hundred trout. Between this river and the Marguerite are the branches of the Bergeronne, which also afford excellent sport. [At the end of this article the tourist will find a list of salmon and trout rivers.] Seal-hunting is a favourite sport with those who resort to these shores; this animal is found in great abundance, and several varieties are here met with. The usual method is to start from Tadoussac with a yawl and canoe, and steer for a spot in the St. Lawrence where the waters of the Saguenay and the flood-tide come together, causing a great commotion. The seal seems to delight in frequenting the deepest water and most turbulent whirlpools, and the object of using the canoe is to steal upon him in the most successful manner. As the seal makes its appearance, the hunter throws a harpoon, to which is attached a line with a buoy; great dexterity is requisite not to upset the canoe; in the event, however, of such an accident, the yawl is at hand to pick up the swimmer, as well as to receive the animal when dead. Another method of capturing them is to pass over in a canoe to a sandy point called "aux Alouettes," and secreting yourself among the rocks, await the game. Hither they resort in great numbers to sun themselves, and they can be picked off by the hunter quite leisurely, provided he does not show himself. Again, if sufficient time is allowed for the tide to ebb a considerable distance from the spot on which they are basking, the sportsman may cut off the retreat of several by running between the water and them, and with a sharp blow on the snout they are easily despatched. Opposite to Tadoussac lies Red Island Reef, a treacherous ledge of rocks, dreaded by inward bound vessels, memorable as being the scene of the shipwreck of Ed. De Caen in 1629, and subsequently in 1848 for the loss of the Gaspé Packet.

— Perhaps the tourist may have a desire to continue his trip down the Gulf and visit GASPE. If so, his best plan would be to take passage in a steamer from Quebec to Percé, and coast along upwards as opportunity offers. For those who purpose visiting this part of the Province, we give the following description of places most worthy of notice :—

The peninsula of Gaspé, the land's end of Canada toward the east, from its geological formation of shale and limestone, presenting their upturned edges to the sea and dipping inland, forms long ranges of beetling cliffs running down to a narrow strip of beach, and affording no resting-place even to the fishermen, except where they have been cut down by streams, and present little coves and bays opening back into deep glens, affording a view of great rolling wooded ridges that stand rank after rank behind the steep sea-cliff, though with many fine valleys between. The inland country is but little settled, but every cove and ravine along the shore is occupied by fishermen, who either permanently reside here, or resort to the coast in summer. This bold and picturesque coast, after running down to the low point of Cap Rosier, on which stands an imposing white brick tower, falls back to the southward and then stretches out into the narrow promontory of Cape Gaspé. Here it was that stout old Jacques Cartier, after battling many days off this cape against the autumnal north-westers, on his first voyage, called a council of his officers, and though anxious to see what lay beyond, bore away on his return to France. When he returned, and at last made land, he found here a tribe of Indians, who appeared to him the rudest he had ever seen ; a branch of the Micmac tribe ; and from their language is derived the name Gaspé, which is stated to mean as nearly as possible the " land's-end." The whole of Gaspé is essentially a fishing district. To the sportsman fond of adventure nothing could be better adapted than a few weeks in Gaspé in the summer, where, with cod, halibut, and mackerel fishing, he could while away the hours, or intersperse his amusements occasionally with the more exciting chase of the whale, the seal and the dolphin. The most abundant of the whale family here is the black whale or "black fish." Formerly these were very numerous, but being timid, and not prolific, the fishermen have already driven them to the north shore of the Gulf, and will probably soon have to follow them farther. Mackerel fishing, when the fish are plentiful, affords great amusement ; two or three fish are cut up in very small pieces, and thrown on the surface of the water from the boat; the fish, allured by this, rise to the surface in myriads. The hooks are then baited with a piece of fresh mackerel or shark, and the line is held either in the hand, or fastened to a rod, and the hauling of them in becomes at last quite laborious. Cod and halibut fishing from boats is performed much in the same way, with the exception of the bait lying on the bottom, the best bait being a small crab. Small boats can be had from any of the fishermen on the coast, but we would recommend the sportsman to join a party in a yawl, and proceed on a fishing excursion for a few days at a time, as he, by that means, will probably come in for the different kinds of fishing in the same trip, to say nothing of the probabilities of a whale or seal hunt, and an occasional shot at some passing sea-bird to add to his collection. Gaspé Bay, to the naturalist, is rich in specimens fantastic in form and curious in structure.

The mud which lies thickly at the mouth of many of the streams is rich in *foraminifera;* on the sandy bottom, flat, cake-like shells called the "Dollar-fish" *(Echinarahnius Atlanticus)* abound. On the more rocky grounds, are immense numbers of various species of zoophytes and bryozoa. Just off the mouth of Gaspé Basin, on a gravelly bank, every stone is coated with millipores ; and starfish, echini, chitons and sea-anemones, in addition to numerous shells, strew the sand-bars and spits in great profusion. The interior of Gaspé has not yet been explored or surveyed ; we must, therefore, content the reader with a description of such places on the coast as are most picturesque and deserve a passing notice.

Cap Désespoir, a rugged, bold promontory, lashed by the full sweep of the Atlantic, is perhaps the most dangerous spot on this coast ; here it was that in 1711 eight English transports, with eight hundred and eighty-four officers, soldiers, and seamen, belonging to Admiral Walker's squadron, met with an awful fate; and the hull of an old wreck is still pointed out, as having belonged to that ill-fated expedition. It is said that fragments of the vessels were driven by the surf on rocks several feet over the level of the sea, so violent was that storm. The spirits of the departed are said to be still seen by mariners flitting about the shores at dusk ; *ignes fatui* of the muddy pools. But probably the sea-weed covered rocks, slimy with the *confervæ* of the ocean, and apparently swaying to and fro, from the ebb and flow of the tide moving the weed, together with the frowning precipice above, and the solitude and silence, unbroken save by the swell of the ocean, contribute a weird appearance to the scene. The nearest village is St. Michel, some seven or eight miles distant.

Close to the redoubted reefs of Cap Rosier, before alluded to, formerly stood " SHIP HEAD," or "The Old Woman," as mariners called it—a fantastic boulder surrounded by deep water, and looming out in calm weather so as to resemble a large ship under full sail,—a veritable phantom ship; hundreds have been deceived by the optical illusion. This well-known land-mark has, however, recently disappeared and toppled over from its base; yet a strange configuration of rock still exists near the shore to which the name of " The Old Man" is given.

In the distance one discerns the fanciful mass called PERCE ROCK, containing a natural arch, under which a fishing smack of ordinary dimensions can pass in full sail. It formerly consisted of two arches, the support of one of which however fell in 1846, resolving the two into one. The summit of it is inaccessible, and nothing but the snowy gannet, the black cormorant, or the silvery gull, has ever sought a footing on this lofty rock. Yet a romantic story is told by the fishermen residing at Percé, about a phantom having been seen during a storm on this rock. It is known as *Le Génie de l'isle Percé*, and the date of its existence runs beyond the memory of man. It is likely that the foundation for this legend can be traced to the vapoury or cloud-like appearance the vast flocks of water fowl assume when seen at a distance wheeling in every fantastic shape through the air, previous to alighting on the summit. The rock is a few miles from Percé, a large fishing village, and one of the *chef-lieux* of the country.

Where La Madeleine runs into the Gulf, horizontal layers of limestone, fretted away all around their base, by the action of the tides and waves, assume the most fantastic shapes—here representing ruins of Gothic architecture, there forming hollow caverns into which the surf rolling, produces a moaning sound, like an unquiet spirit seeking repose. To this spot is attached a legend that in some awful shipwreck here, a father and mother found a watery grave, but their infant son was washed ashore alive, the sole survivor. His infant wailings, blended with the swelling storm, struck the ears of some belated fishermen, who rescued him. Hence the name "*Le Braillard de la Madeleine.*" The noise is still heard in stormy weather; and it, together with the evil repute the whole of this coast lies under, causes the superstitious sailor to the present day to give it a wide berth.

Returning up the Gulf we pass on the south shore, METIS, some 200 miles below Quebec, where is the largest and longest of the government wharves. Here the inhabitants, in addition to the more common kinds of fish, do a small but thriving business in the way of capturing whales, which are of the *hump-back* species, yielding from three to eight tons of oil; they are hunted in schooners and harpooned after the fashion of the regular Arctic whalers. From Métis there is a trail (for road it can scarcely be called) to the Restigouche River in New Brunswick. Métis is a thriving town, and if the Ocean Steamers should eventually call there (as proposed,) it will doubtless become a place of some importance. There are, however, no hotels there as yet.

Proceeding upwards, we come to RIMOUSKI, 180 miles from Quebec, which also has a very extensive government wharf, extending some distance into the river. This village contains an unusual number of handsome houses, and the hotel, kept by one St. Laurent, is first-rate in every respect. The extensive saw-mills and ship-yards give the place a thriving appearance; but the lover of scenery and angling will not remain quiet till he explores the valley of the Rimouski River. As a stream for trout it is unapproachable. A nameless tributary about twenty miles from its mouth, not more than twelve miles long, running through four or five beautiful little lakes, literally swarms with fish, many of them over two pounds in weight. The mountains that hem it in are covered with thick woods, and belong to that range which here boldly swoops down to the St. Lawrence, and form a head-land resembling the beak of an eagle, known by the name of

LE BIC, nine miles from Rimouski. Here is a small village of the same name as the promontory, opposite to an excellent old harbour, where the troops were landed from England in the winter of 1861.

In its vicinity is a small island, which for two centuries has borne the name of L'ISLET AU MASSACRE. A deed of blood marks the spot, and history furnishes the details of the scene. Two hundred Micmac Indians were camping there for the night; their canoes had been beached, and a neighbouring cavern offered an apparently secure asylum to the warriors, their wives and children. Wrapped in sleep, they quietly awaited the return of day to resume their journey. But during the still hours of night the Iroquois had compassed his slumbering foe. Laden with birch bark, faggots, and other combustibles, the Iroquois silently surrounded the cave; the faggots were piled around it; the torch applied. The Micmacs, terror-stricken, seize their arms and prepare to rush through the flames and sell their lives as dearly as possible. But a shower of poisoned arrows mows them down, the tomahawk completes the scene, and history mentions but five, out of the two hundred, who escaped with their lives. The blanched bones of the warriors strewed the cave, and were seen by the Abbe Ferland a few years ago. It has been the subject of an interesting legend by M. J. C. Tache, in the *Soirées Canadiennes*.

TROIS PISTOLES, 140 miles from Quebec, is a place to which the tourist must pay his compliments in passing, not so much on account of its charming scenery and location, as for the pretty river of the same name, where, from a canoe, he will have the satisfaction of seeing half-a-dozen fish at once dart after his fly, the moment it touches the water. About a couple of miles from the shore is a rocky islet called the *Isle of Rosade*, upon which is a wooden cross, with a memorial in French under a glass cover, of the deliverance of forty persons, who, having been attracted on the ice (which very unusually had taken between the island and the shore) by the huge quantity of seals basking there, were cut off from the main land and the island by the breaking up of the ice field with the ebbing of the tide, which commenced to hurry them, near the close of a short December day, down the Gulf, till a bold fisherman, launching a frail canoe at the peril of his own life, rescued them four at a time, and happily succeeded in saving all. The cross was erected by the inhabitants of Notre Dame des Anges, as a silent witness of God's mercy in the hour of peril.

Journeying on, 114 miles below Quebec lies RIVIERE DU LOUP *(en bas)*. This is the eastern terminus of the Grand Trunk Railway, and is another favourite summer resort for sea-bathing and fishing. It is very prettily situated at the confluence of the Du Loup with the St. Lawrence, and contains a more general mixture of English, Scotch and French, than is usually found in the smaller towns of Lower Canada. It commands an extensive prospect of the St. Lawrence, which is here upwards of twenty miles wide, and studded with islands; ships are constantly passing and re-passing, and when, from their great distance, with the mountains in the back ground, all these objects are enveloped in a gauze-like atmosphere of summer haze, there is a magic influence in the scenery. The principal local attraction is a water-fall, about a mile in the rear of the village. At this point the waters of the rapid and beautiful Du Loup dance joyously over a rocky bed, until they reach a picturesque precipice of perhaps 80 or 100 feet, over which they dash in a sheet of foam, and after forming an extensive and shadowy pool, glide onward placidly to mingle with the mighty river. The traveller who wishes to go from Quebec to Halifax, must come to this point to take the Grand Portage Road, which commences here and extends to Lake Témiscouata, a distance of thirty-six miles. The first ten miles of this road are dotted with the cottages of the Canadian peasantry; but the rest of the route leads up mountains and down valleys, as wild and desolate as when first created. The streams, which cross the road continually, abound in trout. On this road is a great curiosity of a geological character, which will repay the curious for their visit. Crossing the road and running in a northerly direction, extending to the width of about two miles, is a singular bed of granite boulders, of every size and form, and while from a portion of them rises a scanty vegetation, other portions are destitute of even the common moss. The appearance it presents is that of the bed of a mighty river, whose fountains have become for ever dry. It has probably been the *grounding place* of some mighty glacier in an early era of the world's history. The Grand Portage Road is all that could be desired, and at the termination of it is the small hamlet of TEMISCOUATA, on the lake of the same name, signifying *winding water*. This is a beautiful sheet of water, of a serpentine course, about twenty-four miles long and from two to three wide. On it are some lovely views, but with the exception of the cluster of houses that forms the hamlet, there is not a single cabin on the whole lake, and the surrounding mountains are the home of solitude and silence. A canoe can readily be had from any of the villagers, and the lake abounds with trout and perch. The outlet of the lake is the Madawaska River which is a tributary of the St. John.

Returning to Rivière du Loup and descending the St. Lawrence about six miles we find KAKOUNA, or as it is commonly spelled CACOUNA, the well-known and fashionable watering place, being to the Canadians what Newport or Long Branch is to New Yorkers. It is one of the finest villages on the St. Lawrence; and from its elevated position, large and comfortable hotels, together with the picturesque scenery in its vicinity, it is visited during the summer season by many thousands of strangers, from the United States and all parts of Canada, in order to enjoy its fine climate, as well as its facilities for sea-bathing.

From Rivière du Loup, thrice a week, a stage runs to

Grand Falls, on the River St. John, which there makes a sudden turn, and becoming contracted to the width of about fifty yards, makes a plunge of perhaps forty feet, mostly in a solid mass. Below this and extending for perhaps a mile, is a succession of falls, which make the entire descent some eighty feet. The water rushes through what might be termed a winding chasm, whose sides are perhaps 150 or 200 feet high, perpendicular, and composed of a bluish slate. Generally speaking, the entire distance from the first fall to the last, presents a sheet of foam, though around every jutting point is a black, and apparently bottomless pool, teeming with fish. There is a comfortable stopping place here kept by a Mrs. Russell. A trip to the falls and back is an agreeable diversion to the sojourner at Kakouna, and will occupy about three days.

On the north shore of the river, some twenty-five or thirty miles from Rivière du Loup, is MURRAY BAY, a small quiet watering place, flanked with frowning hills and wild scenery, with good fishing in a river of the same name. It is a place well adapted to those seeking quiet enjoyment and society during the summer, and owing to its easy access from Quebec is much resorted to. The steamer "Magnet" touches here.

On the north shore of the River St. Lawrence, eight leagues below Murray Bay, is a very lofty cape at a place called LA BAIE DES ROCHERS. On its summit, on which the foot of man never trod, there has existed from time immemorial, in a fissure of the rock, a raven's nest, which is said to have been noticed by the first missionaries who came to Canada. The spot is well worthy of a passing notice from its height and rugged boldness. Leaving this cape behind, we take a glance at Pointe aux Iroquois (near which is a swamp abounding with blueberries of the finest quality), Cap au Diable, and Rivière Ouelle (or "Houel," as it was formerly called) on the southern shore, all interesting in their natural beauty, and possessing each their own legend in the career of the Ghoul of the St. Lawrence (who after all was nothing but a diabolical old Iroquois squaw.) Riviere Ouelle, a station on the Grand Trunk, takes its name from Madame Houel, the wife of a French Controleur General, who was captured by Indians with her little son on their return trip from Quebec in the 17th century. Here are also visible *three curious and inexplicable snow-shoe tracks* deeply incrusted in the solid rock on the beach. Another singular appearance was till recently visible there, though now almost effaced by the action of the tide; it was the marks of the anterior part of two human feet and hands on the rocks. These alone have afforded important aid to the legends of the coast. Similar appearances are stated to exist on the Jacques Cartier River, near Quebec.

Passing by HARE ISLAND, a small rocky island of picturesque appearance, and Seal Rocks, alluded to as affording such excellent shooting, we come to KAMOURASKA, 90 miles from Quebec, a fine flourishing village, containing a gaol and court house; it is pleasantly situated, and was formerly a resort for sea-bathing, but is now eclipsed by other more favored localities.

MALBAIE, opposite to it, on the north side of the river, is another large village with no striking features or attractions except its sea-bathing.

L'ISLET, forty-eight miles from Quebec, a large village, and station of the Grand Trunk, doing an extensive business in lumber, is the next place of any importance. Here theré is an excellent Government wharf stretching out into the river.

All these places on the river, but more especially on the south shore, afford numerous specimens of sea-shells, and will furnish the Conchologist with several varieties peculiar to the Gulf.

GROSSE ISLE, twenty-nine miles below Quebec, is a small island of about two and a half miles in length, but well-known as being the Quarantine Station, where all emigrant vessels are rigorously compelled to stop. To visit this island a written pass must be obtained from the Superintendent or the head Emigration Agent. A small steamer belonging to the Commissioners plies between Quebec and Grosse Isle, and a pass will convey the tourist by it to his destination.

ISLE AUX COUDRES, a pretty well wooded island, where Jacques Cartier anchored on his first voyage, and gave it its present name from the number of filberts growing wild there, and the ISLAND OF ORLEANS, within a few miles of Quebec, styled by Jacques Cartier the Isle of Bacchus, from the numerous vines upon it, called now from its fertility the Garden of Lower Canada, and celebrated as having been formerly used as a place of banishment, are the last islands we pass, and the traveller once more finds himself in the City of Quebec.

LIST OF SALMON AND TROUT RIVERS BELOW QUEBEC.

For the benefit of Sportsmen and Tourists we append a list of the principal Salmon and Trout Rivers below Quebec, with their distance from each other, and such information as may be useful concerning their character and condition. This information is trustworthy. The system of protection adopted by the Commissioner of Crown Lands is not only greatly increasing the number of the salmon, but also enabling them to attain to a larger size:—

From Quebec to Murray Bay is . . . 78 miles
(The river furnishes a few salmon and many fine trout)

From Murray Bay to the Saguenay is . . . 44 "
(The fishing here as well as in the Marguerite has been described.)

River Escoumain . . . . . . 23 "
(Between it and the Saguenay are two branches of the Bergeronne, both furnishing a few salmon and many trout.)

River Portneuf . . . 26 miles
(Plenty of trout and salmon.)
Sault au Cochon . . . . 9 "
(Impassable for salmon, but full of trout.)
La Val . . . . 2 "
(Superior salmon and trout fishing.)
Bersemis . . . . 24 "
(In all its tributaries many fine salmon; between it and La Val are the Columbia, Plover, and Blanche, but all are poor salmon streams.)
River Outardes . . . . 11 miles
Manicouagan 16 "
Mistassimi . . 12 "
Betscie . 3 "
Godbout . . . . 15 "
(A celebrated salmon river, one of the best in the Province.)
Trinity . . . . 15 "
(Good salmon and trout.)
Little Trinity . . . . 10 "
Calumet . . . . . 3 "
Pentecost . . . . . . 14 "
(Not a salmon river.)
St. Margaret . . . . . . 36 "
(One of the best salmon and trout rivers.)
Moisie . . . . 23 "
(Fine large salmon are taken in this river, and it is widely celebrated.)
Trout . . . . . 7 "
Manitou . . . . 35 "
(Good trout fishing; salmon are obstructed by falls.)
Sheldrake . . . . 16 "
Magpie . . . . 22 "
(Furnishes only a few salmon.)
St. John . . . . 5 "
(An admirable salmon stream.)
Mingan . . . . 16 "
(Probably the best river in the Province for salmon and excellent for trout.)

The streams emptying into the St. Lawrence from the south shore, are not worth mentioning as salmon rivers, having been ruined by mill-dams, except those that empty

NOTMAN, Photo.

Lake St. Charles, near Quebec.

into Gaspé Basin, but they all afford superior trout fishing. To Americans wishing to reach this section of country we would say, take the route that will bring you to Boston before half-past seven A.M., for at that hour the boat leaves for St. John, New Brunswick. If you are too late, you may by cars intercept the same boat at Portland, or on its arrival there take steamer to Calais, and thence by rail to Woodstock—where stages connect by the Grand Portage road with Rivière du Loup, and so with all the Lower St. Lawrence. The Boston boat reaches St. John in about 32 hours—fare six dollars, meals extra—consequently extra good.

EASTERN TOWNSHIPS.

Leaving Point Lévi for a trip through the Eastern Townships, the traveller may look forward to enjoying as beautiful a tract of country as perhaps any on the continent, both with regard to mountain and lake scenery, beautiful rivers and fertile valleys. The mountains, wooded generally from base to summit, repose in majesty; and as the mists, with which their summits are not unfrequently crowned, withdraw themselves in folds along their sides, they reveal still more of the beautiful and sublime. Chasms, ravines, and precipices are there, and among their solitudes sublimity reigns. Beautiful lakes lie scattered over the face of the country, bordered here by gentle slopes, there by precipitous cliffs; cultivated fields and wide-spread pastures, with woods interspersed; valleys and plains adorned with farm houses, single or in groups, and beautiful villages. The rocks of the Eastern Townships, geologically speaking, are confined to the two lower series of the *Palæozoic* era. These in Western Canada, from their quiescent condition, give a flat surface ; but here, being disturbed and corrugated, they give origin to a surface beautifully varied with hill and valley. The physical structure of this part of Canada is thus exceedingly complicated. The rocks of which the district is composed abound in mineral ores, and many beautiful varieties of marble. The lakes, however, are its great glory. By them the glens, the mountains and the woods are illumined ; reflected in this pure element the great and stern objects of Nature stand out "a second self." The first settlements in the Townships were made about 1795 by families from Massachusetts, Vermont, and New Hampshire ; and to those enterprising and adventurous pioneers is due, in a great measure, the prosperity their descendants now enjoy. Then "tall pines, blackened by fire, stood as monuments of the prevailing loneliness," and the forest closed like a fortress round the first settler, whose only hope against its shutting him in for life, was his axe. How well that has been wielded, what hardships have been undergone, what fortitude shewn, the smiling homestead and thriving villages of to-day full truly record; and the nearer we approach the frontier lines, the more do the evidences of prosperity increase, as it was there the first settlements were made. The noble River St. Lawrence sweeps past in its course to the ocean, on the north-west of these Townships. Its banks still retain that remarkable boldness which they possess at and near Quebec, till after passing Craig's Road, where there is a remarkable cliff called the Devil's Bit, they lose gradually the boldness of their features till they sink into the flats of La Baie du Febvre. Soon after crossing the Chaudière, the line recedes from the banks of the St. Lawrence, running through the heart of the Townships, and the country begins to assume a peculiarly picturesque aspect. On the upper waters of the pretty river Nicolet we come to BECANCOUR and SOMERSET, forty-one and fifty miles respectively from Quebec, south of which places, in the Townships of Inverness and Halifax, exist a chain of small lakes, not remarkable for their scenery, but very romantic withal from their diversity of hill and dale; these lakes are connected with one another by short rivers and rapids. *Lake Joseph* is in Inverness, on the road to HALIFAX, a small village twelve miles from Somerset Station, which lies on *Lake William*, opposite to the village of ST. FERDINAND. This lake is about four miles long and one wide; it is separated from *Trout Lake* by a deep, crooked river, navigable for canoes only. There is excellent fishing in all these waters; trout of all sizes, white fish, very large eels and pike are abundant. The only accommodation to be had is at St. Ferdinand, where there is no difficulty in obtaining the use of a boat. Near Trout Lake is the small village of MAPLE GROVE, connected with Bécancour Station by a daily stage. The river connecting these lakes has no name, until a little below *Lake Joseph*, it takes the name of Thames, which again further down at Lloyd's Falls—a romantic spot, and where good trout fishing is to be had—is called the Bécancour. Each branch of the Nicolet River is supplied from a lake among the mountains, and throughout this vast tract of country there can be found numbers of streams affording water power which might be turned to profitable account with no great outlay of capital. At a distance of sixty-four miles from Quebec is ARTHABASKA, the junction of the Three Rivers branch of the Grand Trunk Railway, near which, at CHESTER, are two mines very rich in copper ore, and also a lead mine, whilst in South Ham, still further south, is a valuable antimony mine and a lovely lake abounding with trout, called *Lake Nicolet*. Ten miles from the station, in Chester, is situated ROUILLARD MOUNTAIN, forty miles distant in a direct line from the St. Lawrence: yet from the summit of the mountain, on a clear day, that river can be distinctly seen with a glass; the forest between the mountain and the river forms to the eye a most beautiful variegated landscape, and in the months of June or October it appears like a rich green or variegated carpet. Looking towards the south you see a country much resembling North Wales or Switzerland, in regard to scenery; the mountains being a continuation of the great Appalachian chain, and the waters of Lakes St. Francis and Aylmer are clearly visible. *Lake St. Francis*, whence issues the river of that name, is about forty miles north-east of Sherbrooke. It is about fourteen miles long, and from one to two wide; the country around is very sparsely settled, and the lumberer is the chief pioneer of civilization in this part of the Townships. Great quantities of valuable lumber are obtained yearly throughout the whole of this region, and the principal part of the lumber sawn at Brompton Falls, by C. S. Clark & Co., in their extensive mills, is obtained from the forests about this lake. Quite contiguous is *Lake Aylmer*, through which the waters of the above lake pass on their course down the river St. Francis; this is also a pretty expanse of water. About twenty miles south of these lakes, and about forty south-east of Sherbrooke, near the boundary line of the State of Maine, is *Lake Mégantic*, the source of the Chaudière River, whose banks have gained notoriety from the gold discoveries recently made there. The lake is about sixteen miles long, and two in breadth; the country around it is not much settled yet; and still sufficiently remote from the haunts of civilization for the beaver to be found on its tributaries. The St. Francis Indians frequent this section of country, as affording them good hunting grounds, and the lake itself abounds with fish, their principal article of food. This region, however, from the richness of its soil, must soon become peopled. The mountains in the vicinity of the lake have a considerable altitude, but their general aspect is not so picturesque as that of the shores of some other lakes hereafter to be described. The Chaudière River, which issues from this lake, passes through a valley of about 100 miles in length, by about thirty miles in breadth; thus, in its course, draining about 3,000 square miles of land of its redundant waters. Its breadth varies from 400 to 600 yards; its course is frequently interrupted by small, picturesque islands, covered with hardwood timber, which add considerably to its beauty. The banks of the Chaudière are, in general, high and precipitous,—thickly clothed with verdure. The bed of the river is rugged, and often much contracted by rocks jutting out from the banks on either side, which occasion violent rapids. Near the mouth of it are the celebrated falls described elsewhere. This stream has been brought into notice within the last few years, from the discoveries that have been made of gold in its bed, and the washings of its sand-bars and bends. Gold has been known to exist in the region through which it flows for some time, but it never, till within the last three years, was thought to exist in paying quantities. It exists in the quartz rocks scattered through the country, and in alluvial and diluvial deposits. As to the richness of the mines, Sir William Logan says, "the deposits will not, in general, remunerate unskilled labor, and that agriculturists and others engaged in the ordinary occupations of the country would only lose their labour by turning gold hunters." In some places, however, gold has been found sufficiently plentiful to pay the cost of procuring it. Several Companies are organized, and have procured a considerable quantity of the precious metal. *Lake Mégantic*, or *Chaudière Pond* as it was then called, has been rendered memorable in history, as the route by which Arnold, in 1775, accomplished his perilous march through the wilderness up the Kennebec, through Lake Mégantic, and down the Chaudière River to Quebec. The account of his dreary march, and the perils that beset him, are admirably set forth in the "Life of Arnold," by J. Sparks. We are told that a few French were settled some thirty miles from the lake on the river, whose good wishes Arnold assiduously courted, encouraging them to rally round his standard, and to this day some few of the "oldest inhabitants" recount to their children, probably handed down by their fathers to them, the story of the "descent of the Bostonians," as the only great public event that has ever occurred to vary the monotonous incidents of the sequestered and beautiful valley of the Chaudière. Years before, in 1723-'24, the Indians made all their incursions and ravages upon the eastern part of Massachusetts Bay by this route, making a portage from the head of the Chaudière to the head waters of the Kennebec.

Leaving Lake Mégantic, and going due West through a section of country rapidly filling up with thriving homesteads and substantial settlers, we come to Coaticooke, on the Portland branch of the Grand Trunk Railway, nine miles from the boundary line between the United States and Canada. On the river, which gives its name to the village, are a most romantic series of falls, or cascades, extending over a mile in length; these may be reached by leaving the highway between Compton and Coaticooke, at a point of the road distant a mile from the latter village. The river runs through a chasm of eighty or ninety feet deep, the rocks of which are fringed with tangled masses of shrubs and trees, hemlock and spruce predominating, which grow from every crevice and rent in the rocky walls. The falls impress the beholder with sublimity and awe, not a little heightened by the darkness and gloom the chasm adds to the scene. A few miles west of Coaticooke, in the southern part of the Township of Barnston, we come upon a small lake, not generally marked on any of our maps, called *Little Baldwin* or *Pinnacle Lake*. This latter name it takes from a peculiar eminence rising abruptly from the north-east shore of the lake to the height of 1,000 feet, nearly perpendicularly from its base. This is called "PINNACLE MOUNTAIN"; it is wooded for nearly two-thirds of its height, but the remainder, up to its very summit, is entirely destitute of trees, and nearly so of vegetation. The portion that is bare presents little else to the view than great masses of granite rock, thrown together apparently in one of Nature's wildest convulsions. No view in the whole Eastern Townships presents so singular an appearance as this comparatively unknown spot. The bluff, that rises perpendicularly from the water, seems, with its storm-scathed brow, to prop the very heavens, its gray shadows strongly contrasting with the deep blue sky; when seen at sunset through a hazy atmosphere and with a rich glow of yellow and crimson, with clouds touching the outline of the distant hills, it recalls memories of Italian landscapes, and paintings of the fancy viewed in boyhood's days. In the distance the wood-crowned hills fade away; in the foreground the reflection of the mount on the lake renders by contrast the height ten-fold. About ten miles west of this lake lies STANSTEAD, more familiarly known as STANSTEAD PLAIN, a very busy, thriving town, and the business centre of this part of the country. It is beautifully situated on a plain, whence its name, and commands a great range of mountain scenery, extending along the Green Mountains of Vermont, and their continuation into Canada. ROCK-ISLAND is a village situated so near as to form part of Stanstead, although out of the municipality. It is about equi-distant (twenty miles) from five different railway stations, viz.: Waterville, Compton, Coaticooke and Island Pond, on the Grand Trunk; and Barton, Vt., on the Conn. and Pass. Railroads: the latter line, it is expected, will be completed to Newport, Vt., within seven miles, thus affording easier access, although stage connection to all parts from here is very good. The Stanstead, Shefford and Chambly Railroad, whose terminus is now at Waterloo, when extended here will form a link, the want of which is much felt. A stage running from here to Compton, on the Grand Trunk Railway, passes through HATLEY, about a mile from which place lies the lovely little lake of *Massawippi*, or *Tomifobi*, about nine miles long, and from one mile to one mile and a half wide. The scenery of this lake is very picturesque, and a greater variety of fish is to be taken here than in any other lake in the Townships. " Here are to be found," says Hunter, " maskinongé, rock bass, black bass, the sucker, mullet, common pike, pickerel, trout, the eel, and others of less consequence." The access for fish through its outlet, the River Massawippi, which connects the lake with the St. Francis River at Lennoxville, being free from obstacles, may account for the numbers with which it abounds. The shores of this lake are richly wooded, and indented by winding bays and points jutting into the lake, and by arresting the violence of the winds, cause it to present a continuous mirror-like appearance. On the right bank of the lake is a considerable elevation called Blackberry Mountain, a great resort during the season for parties blackberry picking, that fruit growing there very abundantly. A few miles west of Massawippi is LAKE MEMPHREMAGOG, about thirty miles long by a breadth of about two, though in some places it widens into three or four miles. This lake, *the* lake of the Townships, which has been not inaptly styled the Geneva of Canada, lies in a semi-circular form, partly among the mountains, and partly in the valley beyond, which obliquely crosses the northern portion; stretching its southern extremity into the State of Vermont; about one-third of the lake belongs to the United States. Its Indian name was " Memplowbowque," signifying a beautiful expanse of water. The bosom of the lake is everywhere studded with islands, generally covered with woods to the water's edge. The boundary line crosses the lake, running through an island known as Province Island. To do full justice to the scenery of the lake, would require a small volume. The aspect from the water of some of the mountains, which stretch along its western shore, prominent among which is " Owl's

Head," with its conical outline, gives a truly Alpine character to the scene. This mountain is well worthy of an ascent, which takes about two hours, and is a comparatively easy matter. Its height is 2,500 feet above the lake. The top once gained, the toil is never regretted, from the magnificent view obtainable from that elevation. The lake, with all its beauty, lies spread out beneath in a grand panoramic view. and in the far-off south we catch a glimpse, if the sky is clear, of Willoughby Notch, in the State of Vermont. Near Owl's Head are several islands, each of them named after some natural peculiarity, or from some event connected with their history. Of this latter class is *Skinner's Island*, which lies on the eastern shore opposite the mountain. This takes its name, so tradition goes, from a celebrated smuggler in 1812, who, though the object of continual pursuit, invariably disappeared at this point, and being one day hard pressed, the custom house boat, after a long chase, managed to find his empty skiff concealed amongst its rocky shores. No trace, however, could be found of the man; the boat was cut adrift, and he was seen and heard of no more. Ten years later a fisherman, surprised by a sudden squall, was compelled to seek refuge on the island, and so coasted along the shore till he arrived at its northern point, close to which he saw, as the wind tore away the entangled foliage, a large fissure in the rocky side. Mooring his boat he entered it; the cave was some ten feet high, and extended about thirty feet inwards. The first thing that met his eyes was a skeleton, the remains of Skinner, who doubtless sought refuge here, and could not get away again, as his boat had been set adrift. Trailing shrubs and dense underwood had probably covered the entrance, and the spot was comparatively unknown. The cave is an object of interest to tourists, but difficult of access when the wind blows from the west. Another favourite height with tourists is the Sugar Loaf Mountain, from the summit of which the view over

Hatley, Stanstead and Magog Townships, with their numerous farm houses, and patches of woodland here and there, presents a scene most decidedly English in appearance. Directly below the mountain are seen Whetstone Island, Round Island, and Magoon's Point, with its shores beautifully skirted with woods, and its background finely diversified with meadows. The whole eastern shore of the lake, with its gentle slopes and cultivated farms, presents a pleasing contrast to the bold, mountainous aspect of the west. A great resort of families coming to "the lakes" is the pretty village of Georgeville, rendered more agreeable by the daily plying of the little steamer "Mountain Maid." The Camperdown House is the principal hotel; but if accommodation can be procured (and it generally may be had) at a farm house, by all means give it the preference; for however good an hotel may be, and however attentive the host, there is a restraint and a certain feeling of uneasiness, which at once vanishes in a quiet, country homestead. The lake empties itself into the beautiful River St. Francis at Sherbrooke, by means of the River Magog, on which the water power is very great. At the outlet of the lake is the pretty village of MAGOG, where, in the rapids and pools of the stream, the disciple of old Izaak Walton will find splendid trout fishing, the fish weighing from one to six pounds, and he can here, without any inconvenience, throw the fly, which the generality of trout streams debar the use of, from the too close growth of the trees of the forest. A live minnow is also an excellent bait where the rapids are not too strong, and a good, lively worm seldom fails to attract; but the trout is proverbially one of the most skittish of all the finny tribes, though when hungry he is fearless as the hawk. The *tyro* at the sport will often find his gut snapped, his jointed rod broken in pieces and rendered useless, while the simple country urchin at his side, with a coarse line five or six feet long, tied to a short stick, will jerk them out as rapidly as his clumsy hook touches the water. This village, Magog, will shortly be very easy of access, as it is the intention of the Stanstead and Shefford Railway Company to extend their line to this place, connecting, by means of Lake Memphremagog and the steamer "Mountain Maid," with the contemplated terminus of the Conn. and Pass. Railway at Newport, Vt., as well as a direct land connection between the roads, which will be made at Stanstead, thus furnishing another means of communication for the travelling public, between Montreal, the White Mountains, Boston and New York, either for business or for pleasure.

Near the northern extremity of the lake to the west is ORFORD MOUNTAIN, the highest elevation in the Townships, being about 4500 feet in height. From its summit the view may be almost called unique, as you may see the waters of eighteen lakes. At its own base the waters of Orford Lake assume a dark and dreary appearance, probably from the shade of their overhanging mountain, and although there are the same natural accompaniments of scenery as the other lakes possess, yet there is a dreary, desolate appearance about this spot, heightened perhaps by the seemingly interminable forest of pines, which gives an idea of isolation.

The Town of SHERBROOKE, the metropolis of the Townships, is situated at the confluence of the Magog and St. Francis Rivers. The position of the town, rising from the beautiful valley of the St. Francis, on a series of falls, three-quarters of a mile in length, and having a total height of 100 feet, is most romantic, and lying as it does almost equidistant from Montreal, Quebec, and Portland, on the great artery, the Grand Trunk Railway, it is destined to reach a high position of prosperity. Owing to its splendid water-power a number of factories and industrial works are in operation here. Sherbrooke is the most important way station of the Grand Trunk Railway between Montreal and Portland; and from its happy position near to and amidst fine scenery, a very considerable stream of pleasure travel passes through it during the summer months,—a daily stage connecting it with Memphremagog, sixteen miles distant. The jail and court house here are fine buildings, occupying a commanding site.

The St. Francis River, which we touched on before at its source in Lakes St. Francis and Aylmer, receives as tributaries, before reaching Sherbrooke, the Salmon, the Eaton, the Coaticooke, Massawippi, and Magog Rivers, and henceforth assumes more of the character of a river winding on its northward course through a lovely expanse of country to empty its waters into the St. Lawrence, at the head of Lake St. Peter. At East Sherbrooke its banks are sloping, of but a slight elevation, clothed with rich meadow land, and skirted by beautiful elms, overhanging the river side. As we follow its course (and the railway runs beside it up to Richmond) we here see a valley, whose fertility greatly contrasts with the forest we have left. At certain points the level ground is limited to the breadth of the road; on one side we see hundreds of feet below us; on the other we are closed in by a precipice high over our heads. Emerging from a defile we come in full view of the river, on one side a farm-house or little hamlet, on the other a cascade, a factory, or mill, around which are tasteful dwellings, and frequently a pretty village church. From its source to its termination it exhibits one continued series of the most delightful and varied scenery. No one who has ever seen it can forget the valley of the St. Francis, yet among the numbers who yearly perambulate Canada in quest of scenic beauty, how few visit this picturesque spot.

South of Sherbrooke some three miles is LENNOXVILLE, where the Massawippi joins its waters to the St. Francis, and well known as being the seat of Bishops' College, the Oxford of Canada, an excellent Episcopalian institution, provided with a staff of thoroughly sound professors, both in the college and grammar school attached to it, which may not inaptly be called the Eton or Rugby of Young Canada. Near Lennoxville there are some rich copper and lead mines, which have added materially to the increase and prosperity of the village within the last few years.

BROMPTON FALLS, seven miles from Sherbrooke, on the St. Francis, is important principally on account of its large lumbering operations and saw-mills; the establishment of C. S. Clarke & Co. here being one of the largest in the country, and rivalling any of those on the Ottawa. There are a number of other small lakes lying in this vicinity, such as Brompton Lake, Stukely, Brome, &c.; but the scenery of all is so similar, that to enumerate their beauties would be but to reiterate what has already been said, both with regard to their localities and the fishing they afford.

At the junction of the Quebec and Portland branches of the Grand Trunk is situated RICHMOND, ninety-six miles from Quebec and seventy-six from Montreal. It is a place that does not seem to have thriven equally with the other towns of this part of Canada, and yet the whole township in which it lies possesses numerous mill-sites, and there are some valuable copper mines and slate quarries in its immediate vicinity. The Balrath copper mine is only five miles distant, and is in full operation; several others also have lately been opened, and the whole range of rocks here seem highly metalliferous. St. Francis College, standing as it does on a hill, is a building that attracts notice from whichever side you approach Richmond. There is nothing of architectural beauty about it, but its prominence brings it to the notice of every passer by. The institution was founded and is carried on, on unsectarian principles, and has been affiliated with McGill College. Opposite to Richmond, across the St. Francis, and one mile distant, connected by a covered bridge, is the village of MELBOURNE. The river is here characterized by the same beauty which distinguishes it at Sherbrooke, its continuous windings adding so much to the scene, and the contrast between the uninteresting flat country from St. Hyacinthe to this point, where the traveller coming eastwards first strikes this river, is the more pleasing. From hence the St. Francis pursues its northerly course, and the railway leaves its valley and stretches at right angles, east and west, for Quebec or Montreal.

On the Quebec branch, eight miles east of Richmond, is DANVILLE, around which the country is of a highly agricultural nature. Although it is but a small village, there is an academy here fitted up with complete astronomical and philosophical apparatus. The view from the village square looking eastwards towards *Tingwick* is park-like and handsome. From "Claremont Hill," one mile distant, the prospect is beautiful, and at sunrise is perfectly magnificent. A cone-shaped hill called " THE PINNACLE," three miles from the village, rises 1000 feet, nearly perpendicularly above the plain, over which it towers, a landmark to be seen for miles distant. From it Sherbrooke, thirty-six miles distant, can be easily seen with a glass. *Kingsey* Church, twelve miles distant, is visible to the naked eye;—this mountain is a favourite resort for pic-nic parties. A visit to Nicolet Falls, two miles, and Kingsey Falls, seven miles distant, will afford a pleasant excursion, to say nothing of the fish to be found there. From a high ridge on the highway leading from Shipton to Danville, the view perhaps is equal to any in the Townships. Slate quarries have been recently opened in the Township of Kingsey, and the slate is said in composition to resemble the finest Welsh slate.

Leaving Richmond westwards we come to ACTON or Acton Vale, twenty miles distant, where are very rich copper mines, the produce of which is valued at $150 per ton; the facilities for the transportation of the mineral to any part from here are excellent, and these mines rank next in productiveness to the Copper districts of Lake Superior. ROXTON FALLS, six miles distant, connected by a daily stage, is a very pretty place, the *Black River* passing directly through the village, and affording great water-power; it is noted for its manufacture of sole leather, of which large quantities are annually exported. Traces of gold have been found at Acton, but in too small quantities to repay the search. UPTON, six miles further on the railroad, has nothing of any interest, except a number of small rapids on the *White Run*, one mile distant, where there are abundance of trout. The only other feature of interest that we meet with now, the whole country here being very flat, is ST. HYACINTHE, 35 miles from Montreal. This is one of the four cities of Lower Canada, situated on the Yamaska River, which divides it into two parts, and it is possessed of a large local trade. There are a number of really elegant public buildings here, of which the college is the most deserving of notice. It is a handsome cut stone building, over 700 feet in length, and surmounted by a well proportioned cupola, from the top of which a fine view is to be had. The course of studies here is said to be only equalled by the best Jesuit Colleges in France. The chemical laboratory, physical and astronomical apparatus and library, are of the highest order, and every facility is offered for a thorough university education. The Cathedral here is also a fine building. The annual autumn meeting of the Montreal Turf Club is held here, and the pleasure grounds of the Hon. M. Laframboise are a favorite resort for pic-nic parties. The section of country from St. Hyacinthe to Montreal is essentially French Canadian, and the provincial word *habitant* is said to be more strictly applicable to the inhabitants here than in any part of Canada; the proper interpretation of this word, *the people who cultivate small farms*, is fully exemplified here; and from spots by the roadside marking the boundaries of parishes, or perhaps with some trifling legend attached to them, being rendered prominent by large wooden crosses, the mind at once distinguishes the gradual change from the English settlements of the Eastern Townships to the French localities and French farming. As the traveller nears Montreal the towering hills of Belœil, Yamaska, Rougemont, Mount Johnson and Boucherville diversify the view, till, passing through the Victoria Bridge, he finds himself in sight of, and almost at the foot of, that well-known landmark, the mountain of Montreal.

MONTREAL

MONTREAL, the metropolis of British North America, is situated on an island of the same name, about thirty miles long and ten in the extreme breadth, which is formed by a branch of the Ottawa on the north and the St. Lawrence on the south. It is the head of ocean navigation, and the commencement of lake and river communication. The city lies at the foot of a mountain, to which Jacques Cartier, in 1535, surveying with delight the magnificent prospect, gave the name of Mont Royal. An Indian village existed here at his first visit, called Hochelaga, which he described as being encompassed by three separate rows of palisades, having only one entrance, and that "guarded by pikes and staves, as a means of defence against hostile tribes." It first began to be settled by Europeans in 1542, and exactly one century after, the spot destined for the city was consecrated with due solemnities, commended to the " Queen of the Angels," and called *Ville-Marie*, a name which it retained for a long period. Passing down the stream of time to 1760, the date of British possession, we find Montreal a well peopled town, " of an oblong form, surrounded by a wall, flanked with eleven redoubts,—a ditch about eight feet deep and of a

Montreal Harbour with Victoria Bridge.

NOTMAN, Photo.

proportionable width, but dry, and a fort and citadel." Following down another century of time the change is still greater; industry, intelligence, labour, and capital have produced at the present time still more remarkable changes. The city of to-day as seen from any approach, with the mountain in the back-ground, together with its beautiful villas, its glittering roofs and domes (all the latter being covered with tin) tall spires and lofty towers, presents to the beholder a vast and picturesque panorama. It extends in frontage on the St. Lawrence about three miles, and is remarkable for its excellent quays and esplanade or terrace, built of limestone, and presenting, together with the cut stone locks of the Lachine Canal, a display of continuous masonry unequalled on this continent. In this way the city is protected from the annual phenomenon arising from the breaking up of the ice, which frequently is piled up mountains high, and departs *en masse*, crushing against the unyielding quays. The appearance the river presents at that time is very imposing and the sight is unique, for there is no other place where the packing and shoving of the ice are so grandly displayed. For the benefit of those who have never witnessed this spectacle we will attempt to describe it. When the ice has become stationary at the foot of the St. Mary's current (about a mile below the city) the water quickly rises above; and the confined nature of this part of the channel affords a more ready resistance to the progress of the floating masses. It is at this period that the grandest movements of the ice occur. From the effect of packing and piling and the freezing of the whole into a solid body, it sometimes attains a thickness of from ten to twenty feet: when a sudden rise in the waters lifting up a vast expanse of the whole covering of the river, so high as to free and start it from the many places where it rests on the bottom, the vast mass is set in motion by the whole hydraulic power of this gigantic stream. Proceeding onwards, it piles up over every obstacle it encounters, and when forced into a narrow channel the lateral pressure it there exerts, drives the *bordage* up the banks, where it sometimes accumulates forty or fifty feet high. Broken by the massive revetment wall of the quays, the ice piles on the street or terrace surmounting it and there stops; but before the wall was built the sloping bank guided the moving mass to the walls of gardens and houses in a very dangerous manner, and many accidents used to occur. It has been known to pile up against the side of a house more than two hundred feet from the margin of the river, and there break in the windows of the second floor. The "ice-shove" is a sight that a stranger may see only once in a lifetime; and to such as may be visiting the city at the end of March or beginning of April, we would urge a continuous look out as the thaw sets in, to get a glimpse of this grandest of ice movements.

The slopes of the mountain in rear of Montreal are wooded nearly to the summit; but towards the base the forest trees have given place to orchards, that produce apples, pears and plums of the choicest kind. A drive round the mountain is one of the most delightful imaginable, commanding a view of the city and the valley of the St. Lawrence on the one side, and on the other, of the flat country that stretches northward to the confines of the island, washed by the " Back River" or Ottawa, and studded with pinnacles and towers of convents and religious houses. Diverging from this drive the tourist should visit the Protestant or Mount Royal Cemetery on the St. Laurent side, and the French Cemetery on the Côte des Neiges side, near where the road crosses the spur of the mountain that overlooks the city. In the former especially there are some fine monuments, the Molson Mausoleum attracting especial notice; the whole cemetery is tastefully laid out, and from its natural position is one of the most beautiful in Canada.

Montreal abounds in public buildings: the principal of

which is the Cathedral of Notre Dame. This is said to be the largest building in the New World, being 255 feet long and 135 broad; its two towers are each 220 feet high; and its great bell weighs 29,400 pounds. In the north-east tower are a chime of bells, while the north-west one contains the monster bell, which is named "Gros Bourdon," from its deep bass tone. This tower is always open to the public, on payment of a small fee, and from the summit a most magnificent prospect is obtained. In the far distance the blue hills of Vermont tower up; a magnificent plain, stretching miles and miles on either hand, studded with cultivated farms; the splendid River St. Lawrence, two miles wide, intervening, crossed by the tubular bridge, and stretching away like a silver thread in the far off distance. The cost of the edifice was £100,000. The ground floor is covered with pews capable of seating 8000 persons, and the galleries will hold about 2000 more. To see this church crowded, as is the case at the Fête Dieu or Corpus Christi, or on any particular holiday, is a most imposing sight, and one that will never be forgotten by the spectator.

The Bonsecour Market is the next most imposing building, being erected at a cost of £75,000. It has a front of three stories, the upper part being occupied by the various offices of the city. The market is remarkably spacious and convenient in its arrangements, eclipsing anything of the kind on the continent.

The Hotel Dieu, in the northern outskirts of the city, near the village of Mile-end, is well worth seeing; the Convents of Notre Dame, and the Grey Sisters, with St. Anne's Church, St. Mary's College, and the new Church of the Jesuits on Bleury Street, the English Cathedral, the new Trinity Church on St. Denis Street, McGill College, the Court House, Molson's Bank, and Bonsecour Church (the oldest in the city) are all worthy of a visit. The Museum of the Natural History Society, near the Crystal Palace, is well worth seeing, to which admission can be had on payment of 25 cents. The birds here are very well arranged and present a very good collection of Canadian species; and the "Ferrier Collection" of Egyptian antiquities is as perfect as perhaps any on this continent. The whole institution reflects great credit on the Society and the Curator.

But the lion *par excellence* of Montreal, the eighth wonder of the world, is the VICTORIA BRIDGE, the link in the Grand Trunk Railway, connecting (for railway purposes only) the City of Montreal, on the island, with the mainland to the south, giving Montreal an unbroken railway communication of 1100 miles in length, besides connections. It is of iron, on the tubular principle, and is the most remarkable structure of the kind in the world. The bridge has two long abutments and twenty-four piers of solid stone masonry. In the whole history of engineering, no other so truly gigantic an undertaking is met with. It is the creation of the same genius that spanned the Menai Straits; Mr. Robert Stephenson and Mr. A. M. Ross being the engineers of this great work. Each buttress is calculated to withstand the pressure of seventy thousand tons of ice when the winter breaks up and the large ice-fields come sweeping down the St. Lawrence; and the western faces of the piers, that is, those towards the current, which flows through them at a rate varying from seven to ten miles an hour, terminate in a sharp pointed edge, and the fore part of each presents two beautifully smooth beveled-off surfaces. They are so shaped in order to offer the least possible resistance to the ice. The stone used in the construction of the piers and abutments is a dense blue limestone, partly obtained from a quarry at Pointe Claire, eighteen miles above Montreal, and partly from a quarry on the borders of Vermont, about forty miles distant. The blocks of stone are bound together not only with the best water cement, but each stone is clamped to its neighbor in several places by massive iron rivets, bored several inches into each block, and the interstices between the rivet and the block made one solid mass by means of molten lead. The two centre piers are each 18 feet wide—the centre span 330 feet wide, and each of the other spans 242 feet. The total length of the bridge is 9194 feet; the centre tube 60 feet from the surface of summer water; the aggregate length of solid abutments 2600 feet; iron tubing 6594 feet; cost of the bridge $6,300,000. The floor of the bridge rises one foot in 112 from extremities to centre.

Every tourist ought to visit the bridge before leaving Montreal, and if possible go through it on foot. The interior, when viewed by the dim light of a lamp or lantern,—the opening by which you entered growing smaller and smaller in the distance as you approach the middle till it only shines faintly like a pale blue star,—the hoarse rumbling and vibration caused by the slightest sound, striving for escape from its hollow prison,—inspire a feeling almost of awe and reverence. To look from one of the openings in the centre piers on to the St. Lawrence rushing past in one grand stream far below, sweeping under the bridge in eddies and whirlpools, or bursting into little spirts of angry foam as they touch the sharp edges of the masonry—to look along the sides of the iron tube, which taper away at each end in the distance till it seems a mere reed of metal, one cannot but be astounded not only how such a design was ever carried out, but how it could ever have been conceived as practicable.

THE GRAND TRUNK RAILWAY is entitled to notice in connection with the bridge, both on account of its magnitude and importance. Portland, New York and Boston by its means are brought into daily communication with Montreal; while to the West, unbroken connection with the Western States, and every place of importance on the lakes, is afforded. The village of Point St. Charles, the original depot of the Grand Trunk for the city, has entirely grown up in connection with the works and factories of the Company; and with its library and reading room open to its employés, its church and its school house, perhaps no other public body pays so great a regard to the welfare of its dependants. Allans' line of ocean steamers, carrying the mails weekly, connects Montreal with Liverpool, loading in Montreal and sailing from Quebec in summer and Portland (Maine) in winter; and during the season of navigation steamers ply daily to all the principal cities and towns in the Province situated on the lakes and rivers. If the traveller, in the height of summer, fancies that, from the absence of vessels from the harbor at that period, trade is declining, he must bear in mind that the main commerce is in the spring and fall, when the so-called spring and fall fleet arrive, discharge, take in cargo, and are off again; the shortness of the summer season rendering haste indispensable; consequently, the middle of summer sees the harbor comparatively empty of sea-going vessels, but the trade going on is internal.

At Point St. Charles, on the eastern side of the abutment of bridge, is a curiously shaped massive stone, resting on a huge rock, the whole from fifteen to eighteen feet high, and enclosed with a neat white railing, covering about half an acre in extent; this was erected by the workmen of the bridge to commemorate the spot where some 6,500 victims of the Irish ship fever were buried in the fatal summer of 1847, the huts or sheds for the shelter of the emigrants during that season having been erected on the common there. In the small bay below, during the drought of summer, the naturalist will find the small pools abounding with fresh water shells, several species of *unio, limnæa*, etc., not commonly met with, being very numerous here.

One of the best views of the city is to be obtained from the Reservoir behind McGill College, and a visit to the Water Works, near the little River St. Pierre, is a pleasant excursion. A drive out to Lachine by the Upper

Road, through the Tanneries, where is a regular old fashioned French Church, returning by the Lower Road, past the rapids (to be presently described) is very pleasant, both roads being in excellent condition. Lachine is said to have taken its name from the fact of Champlain in 1613 having applied it to the river above the rapids, meaning to point out that it was the way to China, so firmly was he convinced of this in his own mind. It is a pretty little village, divided into Upper and Lower Lachine, and is a great resort in summer for the business people of Montreal, who find it easy of access. There is excellent boating to be had here, and boats can always be procured at the Ottawa Hotel, kept by Mr. Laflamme.

Another beautiful drive is out to the Back River by the Mile-end road, to the village of St. Vincent de Paul and the *Sault au Recollet* and *Priests' Island*, a lovely spot, framed for pic-nics, well wooded and close to a picturesque old mill, where certain conveniences requisite for parties "outing" can be had. From whatever side we approach the city on our return, the scene is magnificent; but perhaps from the river, taking in at one view, the splendid towers of the Cathedral, the tall spires of Christ Church Cathedral, St. Patrick's Church, &c., the elegant front of Bonsecour Market, and the noble old mountain in the background, the *tout ensemble* is perhaps scarcely equalled in America.

The Champ de Mars, in front of the Court House, is a splendid parade ground, and kept in excellent order; and the visitor should not fail to view the exercise and parade of the different regiments in the garrison, which daily takes place here in summer. At night, too, there is generally a military band playing here, and on certain days in McGill College grounds and Viger Square, making those places a fashionable lounge, with its enlivening strains.

Perhaps no other city of its age and size possesses so few historical attractions. In 1668, a party of Iroquois Indians, the inveterate enemies of the French, stealthily landed their canoes on Montreal Island, and massacred indiscriminately, men, women and children, to the number of about 2,000. It, however, was soon peopled again, and continued for a long time the headquarters of the French forces in Canada. After the peace in 1763, it was surrendered to the English, who held it until 1775, when it was taken by the Americans under General Montgomery. In 1763 and 1766, the city suffered from two severe fires, the first destroying 108 houses, the other 90. In 1776 Montreal was again surrendered to the British, reinforcements under General Burgoyne having driven the Americans from the Province. The old fortifications were a substantial quadrangular stone wall, fifteen feet high with battlements, having six or seven gates, and a bastion and redoubt called the citadel, on what is now Dalhousie Square. The name, however, now only remains, *Fortification* LANE having probably run at the foot of the walls. The water front of the Quebec Gate barrack is supposed to be built upon a part of it, and is the only portion left, being, with the old barrack on Water Street, near the Military Hospital, the only vestige remaining of French military power in the city. St. Helen's Island has now taken the place of a citadel, and being not only a strong military camp, but also beautifully wooded, should be visited by the tourist if possible, an order being easily obtainable on application to the Military Secretary or the Town Major.

The immediate vicinity of Montreal affords very little sporting. There is pretty fair pike fishing directly after the break up of the frost at St. Lambert's, opposite the city, and an occasional bass and doré may be taken during the summer; but the incessant traffic of steamers, together with the destruction of fish during the spawning season, has made the fish very scarce. At the foot of Lachine Rapids good fly fishing may be had in summer, but only for white fish and chub, which rise eagerly at a fly. The Back River, eight miles north of the city, affords fair pike fishing in spring, and bass fishing in August; but for a thorough day's sport we would recommend our traveller to take the morning train to Lachine, have a boat ready for him there, or at Caughnawaga, and an Indian to paddle him up to the mouth of the Chateauguay River; there he will find fish enough to fill his basket and afford him all the sport of this part of the St. Lawrence waters, from a maskinongé to a goodly sized perch. No other good fishing ground is to be met with nearer than Boucherville or St. Johns, and for trout than New Glasgow, some twenty-seven miles northwards.

The shooting, too, in the vicinity is one of the things that were. A few snipe are to be had near the Water Works and in the swamps along the River St. Pierre ; also on the road to the Back River, near a place known as *Bougie's Corners*, there is good snipe ground. Woodcock are plentiful in some seasons in the cedar swamps of the island, but the nearest good cock shooting to the city is at St. Andrews, on the Ottawa, and at Norton Creek. A few ducks may be had in the spring and fall near Lachine, taking the islands on the Caughnawaga side ; but the islands at Boucherville afford excellent sport. The absence of any really good sporting on the island, however, is compensated for in the Montreal Fox Hounds, a subscription pack, which would do credit to any Leicester field, and which are ably managed and hunted as long as the season permits. They seldom or never fail to "find," and, meeting always within easy distance of the city, they afford a healthy means of exercise to the lover of the chase. Since the garrison has been here of late years, the races and steeple chases have become quite an institution; and snow shoe clubs, skating rinks (of which the Victoria carries the palm) cricket and base ball, afford plent of amusement to the less ardent admirer of sports. Unenticing as the word " Rink" may be to strangers, few places are more fondly regarded by the youthful portion of the community during winter. Those unacquainted with the glorious Northern sport of skating, can form no idea of the fascination it exercises over those who indulge in it. After once the frost sets in sufficiently severe to form the ice, the rink is seldom empty. At "The Victoria," military bands perform frequently, and fancy-dress entertainments take place two or three times during the season, which are thronged by enthusiastic skaters and spectators. The effect of this stirring crowd, with the inspiring music, brilliant lights, and extra illuminations, render it more like a palace of fairy land than of earth. At *Guilbault's Garden*, on Upper St. Lawrence Street, there is a very good menagerie of wild beasts, and the garden is pleasantly laid out and well worth the entrance fee of 25 cents. With regard to game, great thanks are due to the "Fish and Game Protection Club," for their active exertions in endeavouring to enforce the laws, and it is to be hoped that the fish will again return to their old haunts in the course of a few years.

The visitor must not leave Montreal without paying a visit to the Rapids, and coming over or "shooting" them, as it is called. For this purpose he must take the early train to Lachine, take one of the boats that touch there at about eight a. m., and having accomplished his object, he finds himself again in Montreal by nine, with an appetite for breakfast improved by his morning's outing. The sensation of shooting the Rapids being associated with danger, may deter invalids or nervous persons from attempting the feat; we therefore give a description for the benefit of those who cannot enjoy the scene themselves :—

After taking passage on the steamer at Lachine, the best position the traveller can take is on the upper deck, beside the wheel-house, as being able to view from thence, without being wet by the spray, the whole scene. The steamer will lie to opposite Caughnawaga for two or three minutes, waiting for an Indian pilot to come on board. As great nerve and force and precision are required in piloting, few but Indians can be had willing to undertake the perilous task, which, however, is to them a matter of every day occurrence; use is second nature, and so with them; the hawk's-eye glance of the pilot, when at his post, and the stern determination on his features, are a picture that want the pen of a Cooper to describe. As soon as the vessel feels the influence of the rapids, in an increased swiftness, steam is shut off, and she is carried onwards by their force alone. Suddenly a scene of wild grandeur bursts upon the eye; waves are lashed into spray and into breakers of a thousand forms by the submerged rocks which they are dashed against in the headlong impetuosity of the river. Whirlpools, a storm lashed sea, the chasm below Niagara, all mingle their sublimity in a single rapid. In an instant you are in the midst of them. Now passing with lightning speed within a few yards of rocks, which, did your vessel but touch them, would reduce her to an utter wreck before the crash could sound upon the ear; did she even diverge in the least from her course—if her head were not kept straight with the course of the rapid, she would be instantly submerged and rolled over and over. And here is shown the necessity of enormous power over her rudder. Before us is an absolute precipice of waters; on every side of it breakers, like dense avalanches, are thrown high into the air. Ere we can take a glance at the scene, the boat descends the wall of waves and foam like a bird, and in a second afterwards you are floating on the calm unruffled bosom of "below the rapids." Unlike the ordinary pitching and tossing at sea, this going down hill by water produces a peculiar sensation, which, as the vessel glides from ledge to ledge of rock, feels like settling down. The traveller who runs the rapids for the first time, is almost sure to involuntarily hold his breath at this feeling. Occasionally, too, the vessel seems to be directly running on a ledge of rocks, and you feel certain she will strike; but the skilful hand at the helm suddenly whirls you into a different channel, and in an instant more it is passed in safety. Such is "shooting the rapids;" but no words can convey a fitting idea of the thrilling excitement that is felt during the few moments of the passage. It is one of the sublime experiences which can never be forgotten, and never adequately described. It is in the highest degree creditable to the skill and care of all connected with this branch of river navigation, that no accident of any consequence has ever happened, nor has a single life been lost in this beautiful but dangerous spot.

FROM MONTREAL TO LAKE CHAMPLAIN AND THE RIVER RICHELIEU.

A trip from Montreal to Lake Champlain is a pleasant change, and to the fisherman it always affords pleasing reminiscences. Taking the Grand Trunk Railway, the first place worthy of note which we stop at, after passing through the Victoria Bridge, is St. Johns, twenty-six miles distant, situated at the foot of the navigable waters of Lake Champlain, on the River Richelieu. As far as wood and water can contribute to it, nothing can exceed the beauty of its banks here. A splendid bridge spans the river to St. Athanase, over which, at a distance of six miles, a capital road, through a finely cultivated country, leads to *Scotch Mountain*, a regular cone, from whence can be obtained a magnificent view through the Townships and far into Vermont. For those seeking either pleasure or health, St. Johns is one of the nicest resorts. The fishing here is good; pike, perch, bass, chub, and doré are abundant; boats are plentiful and charges moderate. In the spring and fall of the year there is good duck shooting, and woodcock are abundant in their season. Passing on we reach Stottsville, a small station, near which, in the middle of the Richelieu River, is an island, containing about two hundred acres, and occupied solely by military, no civilian residents being allowed. This is ISLE AUX NOIX, the British frontier military post, strongly defended by a fort called Fort Lennox, garrisoned by some of the R. C. Rifles and Royal Artillery. This was a British naval station and garrison in 1812; and the hulks of ships and gunboats used there at that time are still lying there, and can be seen by the visitor. It was from this station that two American armed vessels were gallantly captured on Lake Champlain 23rd June, 1812. Four miles further on we come to Lacolle, five miles distant from the boundary line, and lying about two miles from Lake Champlain itself. Here may be obtained sturgeon, maskinongé, pickerel, pike, black and rock bass, eels, shad, mullet, catfish of large size, chub, ling, perch, etc. It is an excellent spot for *still fishing*, but trout and salmon are not found here. The shooting is good, including duck, woodcock, snipe, plover and partridge. Close to the station is the battle-ground of LACOLLE MILL, where the American army, commanded by General Wilkinson, in the spring of 1814, numbering upwards of 3000, attacked and completely invested Lacolle Mill, which was defended by Major Handcock with about 180 men, who finally repulsed and drove them back within their own territory. Here also is the ODELLTOWN CHAPEL, celebrated in our local history as the spot where a small band of loyal volunteers defeated four times their number of rebels in 1838, which happened somewhat as follows:—About 4000 insurgents were concentrated at NAPIERVILLE, a small village, four or five miles distant, whence they opened communication with the sympathizers in the United States. A number of their body, however, being captured *en masse* by this mere handful of loyalists, the latter threw themselves into this church, where they awaited the approach of Dr. Nelson, the leader of the revolt, from Plattsburg, with the Napierville party, which they finally repulsed with heavy loss. About four miles distant is the American stronghold, Fort Montgomery, which for some years belonged to Canada, but by the Ashburton Treaty was given up to the U. S.; it completely defends the pass of the lake. Lake Champlain is so called after the celebrated French explorer of the same name, who sailed through it into Lake St. George in 1608. It is one of the most picturesque of inland waters, being 120 miles in length. Almost the whole of it is in the U. S. territory, with the exception of a bay, or rather arm of it, stretching to the north-east, called Missisquoi Bay. The same description applies to it as has been given to the whole lake. "It usurps the business of the canal; floats its heavily laden boats; mirrors numberless hills covered with pine, maple and oak, as well as many farms, all richly cultivated; rolls under a picturesque bridge (the R. R. Bridge of the Vermont Central); enriches broad meadows; laves the threshold of rural cabins, with children sporting beside them in wild glee; yields its treasures to the fisherman; wears upon its bosom the most charming islands; perpetuates in its colour the emerald of summer; receives into its flood a hundred laughing brooks, teeming with trout; and finally waters a broad valley (the valley of the Richelieu) where the yeoman tills his soil in peace, while from many a grove is heard the pleasant singing of the birds." Westward from Rouse's Point some ten or twelve miles, and at a distance of thirty-six miles from Montreal, is HEMMINGFORD, where there is a remarkable huge rent or cleft in a flat rock called "*the Gulf*," at the top of Covey Hill. This chasm is about one hundred feet deep, and about one hundred rods wide; at the bottom of it flows a river, whose water has an inky blackness in appearance, as you look at it over the precipice.

There is also a small lake on the hill, which is well worth visiting. From the top of Covey Hill there is a beautiful panoramic view of the surrounding country, the spires of Montreal being visible with a good glass on a clear day. There are traces of mineral springs in the vicinity, containing sulphur and iron, pointing to extinct volcanic agency. Returning eastwards, and after lingering on the banks of the Missisquoi Bay, the next object of interest in this section is Brome Lake ; lying some sixty miles from Montreal, in a lovely section of country. Near the head of this lake is situated KNOWLTON, a place which bids fair to become a permanent summer residence of some of the Montreal *bon ton;* and certainly a more sequestered and yet accessible spot could scarcely be had. Access is had from Montreal by rail to Waterloo, and thence five miles by daily stage. The fishing in the place is magnificent; and for shooting, the ample cover afforded by the dense growth of reeds at its outlet, with here and there a still deep pool hemmed in with willows and low shrubs, barely admitting passageway for a dug-out canoe to enter, till the lake suddenly expands, showing its surface covered with duck and teal,—altogether make it a most delightful retreat.

Returning again to St. Johns, and taking the course of the Richelieu,—which river differs from almost all others, in becoming narrower the further you descend it, till it discharges itself into Lake St. Peter, after a course of about seventy miles,—we come to *Chambly Canton*, lying between the rapids of the Richelieu river, and the Chambly and St. Johns Canal, distant from St. Johns about twelve miles. This is an old military station, the fort here having been erected by the French in 1711. It is now manned by a few of the Canadian Rifles and the Artillery, but is a great resort for the troops in summer from the garrison of Montreal for target and other practice. CHAMBLY VILLAGE is one mile distant, an old and pleasant village, on the west side of the river, which at this place widens into what is almost a beautiful lake. Although only eighteen miles distant from Montreal by land, yet from the easterly course of the Richelieu, before its junction with the St. Lawrence, the means of water communication are nearly 90 miles! The expansion of the river is called Chambly Basin, nearly of a circular form, embellished by several little islands covered with verdure and fine trees, as ornamentally disposed as if regulated by art. From this basin to its mouth the river retains a uniform width of about 250 yards, and its banks are from eight to twelve feet high. In the vault of the Roman Catholic Church here some of the heroes of the battle-field of Chateauguay lie buried; and Colonel DeSalaberry, called after that memorable engagement the "Canadian Leonidas," Seigneur of Chambly, sleeps his last sleep here. A few miles further we come to the little village of St. Charles, memorable for being the spot where in '37 a cap of liberty and pole were erected, and where the insurgents had assembled and fortified their position so obstinately, that the works had to be stormed, and every house in it but one was burned. ST. DENIS, a little further, has obtained unenviable notoriety from the murder of Lieut. Weir, who had been sent overland to Sorel from Montreal with despatches, and wishing to join his regiment, which was on its route to St. Denis, in eager haste, arrived there too soon, and thus fell a prisoner into the rebels' hands, who barbarously and brutally murdered him, and threw his body into the Richelieu.

The tourist now directs his steps to a mountain which he has seen towering up; this is BELŒIL MOUNTAIN, twenty-one miles below Montreal, and about twelve from Chambly, and three miles from the Belœil station on the G. T. R. It is known also as Rouville, and Mount St. Hilaire. The village of Belœil is situated on the north shore of the Richelieu, which having been crossed, a very picturesque road conducts the traveller to the southern base of the mountain.

The road winds through a deep grove of maples, and the ascent has been so far improved as to admit of ladies accomplishing it with ease. Soon the traveller reaches a lake of singular formation, to which, though there is an outlet, through which the water is constantly flowing, so as to turn several mills, there is no perceptible inlet. It is supposed to be the crater of an extinct volcano. The lake abounds with fish, of which perch of a goodly size are the most numerous; but fishing is difficult there on account of the scarcity of boats. The best method is to construct a float of branches and brushwood, from which to fish on the margin of the lake. At a short distance onwards commences the ascent of the peak, which is studded at intervals by fourteen wooden crosses, each of which bears an inscription having reference to our Saviour's journey to the place of his crucifixion. Some years ago a dignitary of the Church of Rome, the Bishop of Nancy, visited Canada, and caused a small oratory to be erected on the very crest of the mountain; this was surmounted by a huge cross, covered with bright tin and thus rendered visible from a great distance. It was destroyed, however, a few years ago, but is again to be erected. From the summit of the mountain, whose height is from 1,100 to 1,400 feet above the river, when the state of the atmosphere is favorable, the visitor can see about sixty miles in each direction; and the windings of the St. Lawrence, the shining waters of the Richelieu and Lake Champlain, and the distant range of the Green Mountains, present a panorama that amply repays the beholder for all the fatigue he has undergone. A large hotel, capable of accommodating 200 guests, was built here by the enterprising Seigneur, Major Campbell, but, unfortunately, was totally destroyed by fire.

Trains from Montreal stop at Belœil Station, several times a day, so that there is no difficulty in returning to the city if desirable, or of leaving for some other direction.

FROM MONTREAL TO QUEBEC.

There is very little really worthy of notice, and very few objects that attract the attention on the trip from Montreal to Quebec. As the steamers always leave, however, in the evening, it is better for the tourist to choose a moonlight night for what little there is to see. Leaving Montreal to proceed down the river we pass *Longueuil*, a small village, on the south bank, and the summer residence of many of the citizens of Montreal, with which it is connected by means of a ferry-boat. It is memorable in history for the repulsion of General Carleton in 1775; and a little further on the north shore is *Longue Pointe*, where is a fine building, the Convent of the Sœurs de la Providence. At a distance of nine miles from the city we see *Pointe aux Trembles*, founded in 1674; here is one of the old French Churches, built in 1704;—soon afterwards we find ourselves among the islands of Boucherville. These islands are mostly low and flat, with very shallow water among them, and a thick growth of reeds and other water weeds, affording excellent duck shooting and pike fishing, but wanting in scenery from their extreme flatness; here it is that the ice grounds or settles on the break up of the winter, causing the inundation which almost always annually takes place above;—and at a distance of 15 miles we pass Varennes, one of the most prettily situated places between Montreal and Quebec; it lies with the St. Lawrence in front and the Richelieu in its rear. A steamer runs between it and Montreal four times a week, and it is rising into notice from the mineral springs situated about a mile from the village. At a distance of forty miles we pass *Berthier*, on the north shore, opposite to the entrance of the Richelieu and to numerous islands similar to those of Boucherville, till five miles further down, at the junction of the Richelieu, we arrive at SOREL, which, though a small town, is the first stopping place for steamers to Quebec. This place is also called William Henry, after William IV, who, when in the navy and lying off Quebec, visited this place, coming up in his vessel to Lake St. Peter, whence he took a small boat upwards. It is built on the site of a fort, constructed in 1665 by De Tracey, and was for many years the summer residence of successive Governors of Canada. This is the wintering place of most of the river craft and steamers that ply between Quebec and Montreal. There is splendid snipe shooting in the neighbourhood in October, and very good fishing all through the year among the numerous islands which here stud the surface of the river. About five miles further down the river expands into a vast sheet of water, about twenty-five miles long and nine miles broad, which is known as Lake St. Peter. It is for the most part quite shallow, except in a narrow channel, which has been artificially deepened, so that the largest sailing vessels and the Canadian and Liverpool steamers pass up and down without difficulty. This channel, however, is very intricate, and requires to be marked out with buoys, and fir-poles stuck in the mud, with part of the green tuft left on their tops. It affords very good pike fishing, and enormous quantities of eels can be taken here; there is also good duck shooting along the margin of the lake in the bayous or inlets, which are numerous on its shores. Lake St. Peter in stormy weather is a dangerous place, both for rafts, which are apt to get broken up here and their timbers parted asunder by a storm, and for large vessels, from its shallowness, in event of their getting out of the channel. In passing through this lake the traveller will be almost sure to see several rafts on their way downwards, floating lazily along with the current, or, if there be any breeze, with two or three huge pieces of canvass spread out from an upright fir-pole in lieu of mast or sail. On each of these rafts a shed is built, or "shanty," as it is called, for the raftsmen's sleeping quarters, several weeks

F

not unfrequently passing before the raft reaches its destination. Some of the men rig out their huge unwieldy craft with gay streamers, which flutter from the top of the poles, presenting a rude *gala* appearance. When a number of these rafts are lashed together, belonging perhaps to the same owner, they make as it were a floating island half a mile wide and a mile long, forming a very picturesque appearance ; and when the voices of these hardy sons of the forest and the river join in some of their Canadian boat songs, really "keeping time" with their oars, the wild music, borne by the breeze over the water to the traveller's ear, as his steamer threads its way past them, has a charming effect. Passing the mouth of the River St. Francis, which flows in from the Eastern Townships, and near which is a settlement of the Abenaquis Indians, we arrive at the City of THREE RIVERS, situated on the north shore of the St. Lawrence, at the mouth of the St. Maurice River, which here separates into three channels (whence the name of the city is derived) and lying about mid-way between Quebec and Montreal, being about ninety miles from either of these two places. It ranks the third city in the eastern section of the Province, and carries on a very extensive trade in lumber; the Government improvements on the St. Maurice River of late years having given great advantages to the lumbermen, in obtaining an easy access to market. The River St. Maurice and its tributaries water a territory of over 50,000 square miles, exceedingly rich in lumber. Large quantities of sawn lumber are manufactured here for the West Indian trade. There are also foundries, or as they are called "forges," in full operation here, which have turned out excellent railway car wheels, and are celebrated for their box-stoves. The iron used is principally bog-iron, and one of the foundries, known as the "St. Maurice Forges," a few miles back of the city, on the right bank of the river, has been in operation for over one hundred years. They were established by the French in 1737; at the conquest of the Province the right of the French King devolved on his Britannic Majesty, and these forges have been let to private parties, who have worked them very successfully. Three Rivers is the See of a Roman Catholic Bishopric, and the Cathedral is a stately edifice and one of the finest in Canada, well repaying a visit. Comparatively little is known of the St. Maurice, or of the country through which it flows, but in the section of country lying between it and the Saguenay innumerable quantities of small lakes occur, varying from two to a hundred square miles. A trip up the river will amply repay the tourist, both for scenery and for sport, the waters teeming with fish, and the woods with game of every description. The banks of the river are generally high. About thirty miles up, the River Shawenegan joins the St. Maurice, and a little above its confluence, though on the St. Maurice, the stupendous *Falls of the Shawenegan* are met with, one hundred and fifty feet perpendicular, and second only to Niagara. The general mode of accomplishing a visit to them is by engaging a canoe with voyageurs at Three Rivers. They will ascend as far as the Portage des Grais, where the tourist, having arrived by vehicle, will meet them, as a boat at the spot without previous arrangement cannot always be relied on. After entering the canoe, the Isle aux Tourtes is passed, and on approaching within about a mile of the falls, they can be distinctly seen through the tops of the highest trees. Notwithstanding the numerous rapids below the falls, there is much less difficulty in ascending than might be expected; for while a current runs down the mid-channel, at the rate of five or six miles an hour, there are opportunities of taking advantage of an eddy on either side running up, by shooting rapidly across the main stream. When the water is high in April and May, there are three distinct falls unconnected with each other, and meeting in a large basin. The rocks that separate the fall are respectively called "*La Grand-Mère*" and "*Le bonhomme.*" In the chasm below, where the waters of the different falls meet, the scene is sublime and terrific, giving the appearance of an enormous mass of snow violently agitated. There are large fissures in the precipitous rock, into which the waters are driven with great force, and which rebound again in sheets of spray with a deafening sound. Immediately above the falls the current is unbroken and quiet, though very rapid, as may be observed on seeing a huge log suddenly dip one end and wholly disappear on approaching the edge of the precipice. These falls have been rendered memorable for the melancholy drowning of the son of the late Governor General, which took place there a few years ago. Proceeding up the river the traveller arrives at the *Portage des Hêtres*, or Beech Portage, where he has to leave the canoe and walk round the rapids; resuming it again, a few miles will bring him to the FALLS OF THE GRAND-MERE, which, though not equal to those below them, are well worthy of a visit. The length of the St. Maurice is estimated at about 400 miles, though nothing definite is known respecting its head waters. From GRANDES PILES to LA TUQUE there is a steamboat plying, but above that, some seventy or eighty miles from Three Rivers, so many rapids and cascades occur that, with the requisite portages, the navigation becomes tedious and dangerous. The forests abound with deer and caribou, and good sport can be relied on by those desirous of hunting; but the disciple of St. Hubert must be prepared to make his couch of hemlock boughs, and bid farewell to civilization for the time being. Several Indian hunters of the tribe of the Algonquins can be obtained at Three Rivers, who for a gratuity will take the sportsman safely through the otherwise inextricable mazes of the bush; and a week of this life late in the fall or early in the spring will amply repay in game the hardships of a "tramp in the woods."

It is not improbable that the sportsman may, in the proper

season, and with proper Indian guides, meet with the largest of the deer tribe—the Moose *(Cervus Alces.)* The chase after this animal affording such excellent sport, and withal leading through the wildest and most sequestered fastnesses of the woods, we cannot omit a slight description of the sport. It is generally hunted when the snow is deep, and sufficiently crusted with ice to bear the weight of a dog, but not of a moose itself. Five or six men provided with knapsacks, containing food for as many days, and all necessary implements for "camping" out at night, set out in search of their game. Having found their animal they will wait till day-break, when the dogs are laid on, and the hunters wearing large snow-shoes follow as closely as possible. The deer does not run far before the crust on the snow, through which he breaks at every step, cuts his legs so severely that the poor animal stands at bay, and endeavors to defend himself by striking with his forefeet, till the arrival of the hunters ends his career. "Frank Forrester," the great authority on American sport, cites an instance of a friend of his "killing seven of these glorious animals on the River St. Maurice, in the rear of the pretty village of Three Rivers, all of which he ran into upon snow shoes, after a chase of three days." The following description of a hunting party's encampment is so spirit stirring that we cannot pass it by:—"The first thing to be done on a tramp is to encamp the first night, since it is rare that a single day's march carries the sportsman to the scene of action. The arms are stacked, or hung from the branches of the giant pines around the camp; the snow is scraped away from a large area, and heaped into banks to windward; a tree or two is felled and a huge fire kindled; beds are prepared of the soft and fragrant tips of cedar and hemlock branches; and the party gathers about the cheerful blaze, while the collops are hissing in the frying pan, the coffee simmering in the camp kettle, and the fish or game—if the Indians have found time to catch a salmon-trout or two through the ice, or the sportsmen have brought down a brace or two of Canada grouse—is roasting on wooden spits before the fire, with the rich gravy dropping on the biscuits, which are to serve thereafter as platters for the savory broil. Then comes the merry meal, seasoned by the hunter's Spartan sauce—fatigue and hunger; and when the appetites of all are satisfied with forest fare, the composing fumes of the hunter's pipe succeed, replenished with the Indian weed 'that briefly burns,' and such yarns as are spun nowhere, unless it be in a forest camp, are told. It is a sport for men, not to be essayed by babes or sucklings. No particular fitness is required, except stout thews and sinews—to be long-winded—and accustomed to field exercise."

Opposite to Three Rivers is Doucet's Landing, the terminus of the Arthabaska and Three Rivers branch of the Grand Trunk Railway, thus keeping this section of country easy of access when the frost of winter has closed the river to all navigation.

THREE RIVERS may be said to be at the head of tidewater. In winter great quantities of "tom-cod," a small and very palateable fish, are taken through holes cut in the ice, near the city, in baskets let down and baited with offal; these being suddenly drawn up at intervals of a few minutes, enclose some ten or a dozen of the fish, which are particularly numerous here, probably from the junction of the fresh and tide-water, affording fine feeding-ground. Continuing our journey down the river, we pass Batiscan, Ste. Anne, and the Jacques Cartier River (formerly a good salmon river, and beginning, under the auspices of the Fish and Game Glub of Quebec, to again furnish sport), we find the land rising on the river banks, presenting a more bold and picturesque appearance as we near Quebec. St. Augustin and St. Antoine, two pretty villages, are soon passed, and the mouth of the Chaudière is the next object of interest. Here, some twelve or fifteen miles from Quebec, in the deep seclusion of a thick wood, are the Falls of the Chaudière, a river which, flowing through the auriferous district of the Eastern Townships, and abounding during its course of one hundred miles in rapids, precipitates itself upwards of a hundred feet into a rocky and chaotic basin, where, during the spring freshets, the roaring of the waters and the fantastic cliffs and ledges on either side combine to make a very deep impression on the mind. In consequence of the cavities and chasms in the rocks, the foaming fury of the fall is increased, and the spray evinced by this produces all the colours of the rainbow in the sunshine. The deep green foliage of the woods overhanging, the roar of the cataract, and the solitude of the place, especially as you emerge suddenly from the forest fastnesses, on the scene, produce a strong and vivid impression, not soon to be forgotten.

Below this, and nearly opposite to Quebec, we pass POINT LEVI, or LEVIS, on the Lauzon or southern shore, with its river *Bruyante* (so called from its roaring being heard in Quebec before a south-easterly storm), or *Etchemin*, as is its proper name. Lévis has grown into importance within the last few years, as being the depôt of the Grand Trunk Railway for Quebec. The difficulty of crossing the river in winter from this point, has also greatly contributed to render this place worthy a passing notice. To those who do not know Quebec in winter, it is scarcely possible to convey any idea of the interest that is felt in the formation of the "ice bridge" from Point Levi to the city. When the ice does not take between the two shores, there is often much difficulty in crossing the river. The stream is then full of masses of ice, varying in size from a few feet square to many hundred feet, through which the traveller is taken in a heavy canoe. Should the boatmen be fortunate enough to strike a good crossing and get clear water the journey is quickly made, and is not unpleasant. This, however, is not always the case, and you may be tossed about for hours on the ice, landing at last far from your destination. But, with all these perils, it is seldom a canoe is lost, and a fatality on the passage is hitherto unknown. This "canoeing" employs numbers who would otherwise be idle, and is quite a science of its own. When the ice bridge takes, a road across is soon formed, which generally holds till April. The old means of transit by canoe, however, is almost one of the things of the past ; a strong iron-plated steamer, the *Arctic*, having been built specially for use as a winter ferry when the ice bridge is not formed. During the summer months the ferry boats make continuous trips. The town originally was named after Henri de Lévis, Duc de Ventadour, a lineal descendant of the house of Israel, if a family picture quoted by l'Abbé Ferland in his *"Cours d'Histoire du Canada"* is evidence of such matters. The churches, both English and Roman Catholic, nestling up among the hills, give a pleasing and finished appearance to the scene. It has been noticed in history as the point from which Quebec was assailed several times, though unsuccessfully.

M. De Gaspé in his " Les Anciens Canadiens" has rendered this spot noteworthy, from a tradition respecting an iron cage which was dug up here and exhibited in 1850, falling eventually into the hands of Barnum, in whose museum the "Point Levi relic," as it was styled, remained on view a long time, where next to the woolly horse, the Aztecs, and other modern wonders, it attracted considerable attention. It is supposed to have been the instrument in which Marie Corriveau, the poisoner, called by LeMoine the Canadian Lafarge, expiated her crimes in 1763 by being publicly starved to death, fastened in this cage to a gibbet erected close by the spot where the temperance monument now stands.

Another mile and the traveller finds himself in Quebec, ready for another tour, which can be taken from Point Levi through the Eastern Townships back to Montreal again.

The Habitant—Berry Gatherer—(by Kreighoff).

NOTMAN, Photo.

A peculiar feature of the scenery on the river, the whole way down from Montreal to Quebec, and still further as far as Rivière du Loup, are the numerous white cottages dotting its banks at a few arpents distance from each other, while behind them in the background the woods and hills stand out in almost their primeval state. These are the dwellings —the little farms of the Canadian *habitant;* the principal roads of each parish run parallel with the river, and are completely lined with these rural dwellings. As a class the habitants are devoted to agriculture; entirely destitute of enterprise they tread in the steps of their fathers. There is perhaps no more cheerful, happy or contented being in existence than the habitant; his little farm supplies him with enough to live upon, and he never gives himself anxiety about to-morrow. The men like the old French peasantry wear the old fashioned *capot*, and on their feet mocassins made of cowhide,—the women jackets of bright colors, and on their heads either a cap or straw hat, made in the gipsy fashion. They are fond of social intercourse, and spend a goodly portion of their time in visiting each other. Those who live in the vicinity of Quebec or Montreal, partly supply those markets with vegetables; and it is not an unusual thing for the tourist in perhaps one of the remotest nooks he may be penetrating in search of scenery, and thinking himself far removed from man, to come suddenly upon one of this race, trudging along staff in hand, and a bundle of baskets on his back, which he will shortly fill with berries—raspberry, blueberry, or strawberry, to be taken perhaps many a mile to market, and happy in his simplicity humming to himself the burden of some old Norman song brought here by his forefathers years ago. In the habitant's house the walls are always well whitewashed—the place scrupulously clean, with flowers in the window. You may speak execrable French —many English unfortunately do—and make mistakes that would excite the risibilities of a saint, yet you never see a smile on his face, nor on the faces of his children. For generations their character has undergone no change, their cheerfulness and primitive simplicity have been equally enduring. Truly it is pleasant to study the sunshine of the human heart, which beams out on these rugged spots of Nature's handiwork.

THE WILD FLOWERS OF LOWER CANADA.

The quantity of wild flowers to be found in the environs of Quebec, rich in perfume and wild beauty, are a miniature collection of the genera distributed through the Lower Province generally. They have been so ably dwelt on in works more especially devoted to the natural history of the Province, that we could not do Nature justice by enumerating them here; but we quote from that pleasant writer, Mr. Lemoine, the following: "A stranger," says he, "landing in this country is much surprised to find the flowers which he has carefully cultivated in his garden at home growing wild at his feet; such as Dog-tooth Violets, Trilliums, and Columbines;—the *Trillium*, for which I paid three shillings and sixpence when in England, positively growing wild. I could scarcely believe that I had a right to gather it; having paid so much for one, I felt that it was property, valuable property, running wild." After the Purple Trillium has done flowering we have the Painted Trillium in the woods: the *Trillium grandiflorum* is abundant at Grosse Isle. The spotted leaves and the bright yellow flowers of the Dog-tooth Violet, fully recurved in the sunshine, contrast beautifully with the fresh green grass of the banks on which they are usually found. The *Smilacina bifolia*, sometimes erroneously called the White Lily of the

Valley, the *Smilacina trifolia,* the *Dentaria,* and the *Streptopus roseus* or Twisted Stem, a rose-colored flower, bearing red berries in the fall, are abundant. There are also the Mayflower, the *Hepatica,* and *Symplocarpus,*—thickets crowned with *Rhodoras* in full bloom—a bush a few feet high with superb rose-colored flowers ;—the *Kalmia angustifolia* or American Laurel, and the *Cypripedum humile,* the beautiful Ladies'-slipper Orchis, the Bunch or Pigeon-berry, the Brooklime Speedwell, the Blue-eyed Grass, the Herb Bennet, the Labrador Tea, the *Oxalis stricta* and *Oxalis acetosella* (Woodsorrel) one with yellow, the other with white and purple flowers ;—the Ragwoot, the Anemone, so famous in English song, principally represented by the *A. Pennsylvania,* bearing large white flowers ;—the *Corydalis,* the *Smilacina racemosa,* resembling Solomon's Seal. Here we light upon a lovely tulip bed ; no, 'tis that strangely beautiful flower the Pitcher Plant, *Sarracenia purpurea,* so effective in the cure of small-pox ;—the Forget-me-not, *Œnothera* or Evening Primrose, the False Hellebore, the one-sided *Pyrola,* the Bladder Campion, the Sweet-scented Yellow Mellilot, the White Yarran, the Prunella with blue flowers, the St. John's-wort with its yellow clusters, the object of fair maidens' pursuit on midsummer eve ;—the Willow Herb, the Yellow Lily, the Partridge-berry, the Indian Pipe, the Ladies' Tresses, the Purple Eupatorium, the Snake's Head ;—and hundreds of other most beautiful flowers, each of which could hold a place in an English conservatory or flower garden, are scattered over the sequestered heights and swampy marshes of the woods of Lower Canada.

UP THE OTTAWA.

Leaving Lachine in the steamer "Prince of Wales," on the arrival of the early morning train from Montreal, we pass, about two miles up the bay, the Isle Dorval, formerly the residence of Sir George Simpson, the Governor of the Hudson Bay Company, and latterly of General Williams; we then steam along the north shore of an expansion of the St. Lawrence, called Lake St. Louis, into which, through a narrow passage, part of the waters of the Ottawa flow; and it is curious that the waters of the two rivers for some distance run side by side, as if refusing to mingle, and the line of demarcation can be clearly traced; the St. Lawrence being of a greenish hue, while the Ottawa furnishes a slightly olive brown tint. The junction of the two mighty rivers seems to have caused the formation of the Island of Montreal, and the others adjacent to it. Two distinct branches of the Ottawa winding between Isle Jesus, Isle Bizarre, and the main continent, rejoin the St. Lawrence at Repentigny, whilst another and the greatest, rushing among a cluster of islets and rocks, lying in the channel between Isle Perrot and St. Annes, mingle with the waters of Lake St. Louis.

The Ottawa or "Uttawas," has never been explored up to its head waters. It is known to flow from Lake Temiscaming, and to have a course thence of at least five hundred miles, but how much further north it takes its rise is unknown. Formerly from forty to fifty canoes proceeded yearly from Lachine with articles of traffic, and ascended the Ottawa for about 300 miles, whence they were carried by *portages*, and then passed through French River to Lake Huron. Here they were met by messengers called "Coureurs des Bois," who brought the furs from the Indian hunting-grounds, and exchanged the peltries, as they were called, for European goods. The Ottawa was the grand route of these fur-traders, and was little known, except to those employed in that business.

At the end of the lake, or rather at the entrance of the Ottawa, lies the picturesque village of Ste. Anne, distant twenty-one miles from Montreal, clustering round an old church, which owes its existence and support to the contributions of the Canadian voyageurs, who never omit to pay their offerings to the shrine of St. Anne, before engaging in any enterprise. Here it was that Tom Moore composed the popular Canadian Boat Song, and many who have never seen and never will see "Uttawas tide" have sung about it till it has become almost a household word. A massive bridge crosses the river here, supported on sixteen stone piers, and built for the central section of the Grand Trunk Railway, which has a station here. There are also a set of locks here for vessels to avoid the rapids, which are formidable, more from their shallowness than their velocity. A number of small islands are scattered about, and there is excellent shooting and fishing in the vicinity; here also is the favorite resort of yachts from the Lachine or Beauharnois Clubs, the expanse of Lake St. Louis affording ample room for their movements, and the head of it, Ste. Anne, an excellent rendez-vous for the crews.

Proceeding onwards, about two miles, at the western extremity of the island of Montreal, we see the ruins of two old towers or forts, constructed to keep off the attacks of hostile Indians, and near them the remains of a larger fort taken from the French, and bearing the marks of war in its walls. The expansion of the river here, probably caused by the narrowness of its outlets, bears the name of LAKE OF THE TWO MOUNTAINS, and the hilly character of the scenery, clothed to the water's edge with the richest verdure, presents more the appearance of an inland lake, than the banks of a river. The higher of the two hills, from which it obtains its name, is called Calvary, and is held sacred by the Canadians and the remnant of the Indian tribes living at its base, consisting of Iroquois, Algonquins, and Nepissings. Near this lake, on the north-east, are ST. EUSTACHE, ST. BENOIT, and STE. SCHOLASTIQUE, all of them, but especially the former, celebrated in the history of the rebellion of '37, as being one of the points at which the rebels made their headquarters. Sir John Colborne attacked it, and was completely successful, though with great destruction of life and property. The handsome church was burnt, the presbytère and about sixty of the principal houses. One of the leaders was killed near the church, and numbers fell, burnt, suffocated, or shot. At St. Benoit, the people profiting by the destruction of St. Eustache, advanced with a flag of truce, and 250 of the insurgents unconditionally surrendered, and were paroled. This may be said to have terminated the insurrection, as far as Lower Canada was concerned. The banks of the Ottawa River, generally speaking, are low, with hills rising in the distance some three or four miles inland; and from Lake St. Louis up to Carillon the banks are higher than elsewhere, if we except Grenville, to which place from Carillon runs a canal formed to overcome the impetuous rapids called the Carillon, "the Chute à Blondeau," and "Long Sault." Opposite to Carillon, twenty-seven miles from Ste. Anne, at Point Fortune, is the diverging point of the boundary line between Upper and Lower Canada, the Ottawa from here upwards being the natural division between the Provinces. Two miles from here lies the pretty village of St. Andrews on the North River, and LaChute, seven miles further east. These villages seem to have taken their names from Fort Carillon and its surroundings near Lake Champlain.

At Carillon the traveller leaves the "Prince of Wales" and is conveyed by railway through a prettily wooded tract of country, twelve miles to Grenville, where the land becomes very hilly, rising abruptly from the water's edge. Opposite to this village, at the head of the Long Sault rapids, is Hawkesbury, where we meet with the first of the large lumber establishments, which have been the means of developing the whole upper portion of the Ottawa, whose waters would probably otherwise have rolled for years to come through a dense wilderness. These mills, which are three in number, are principally supplied from the Rivers Gatineau and Rouge, and manufacture on an average 27,000,000 feet, board measure, per annum. To give an idea of the vastness of these lumbering establishments to those unacquainted with that line of manufacture, we append a description of these mills; for the description of one answers for all others in its general outline. They belong to the Hon. John Hamilton & Brother, who have paid the greatest care to secure the comforts of the people under their control, and the whole village bears signs of opulence and order. The dock is capable of containing 40,000 saw logs; the mills contain ninety-two vertical saws, nineteen circular saws, fourteen butting saws, driven by sixty-three water-wheels; fifteen hundred saw-logs are manufactured in twenty-four hours, and one hundred and sixty-five men and boys are employed in and about the mills. These are divided into day and night workers, alternately working for twelve hours each, so that during the summer months the mills never cease running. Of agricultural produce there is expended 750 tons of hay, 25,000 bushels of oats, 5,000 bushels of turnips, 6,000 bushels of potatoes, 1,000 barrels of pork, 9,000 barrels of flour, and 2,000 barrels of oatmeal in the woods. So that 2,000 tons of agricultural produce is consumed by this firm alone. This shows what an important branch in the industrial economy of the Province the lumber business is, and what vast resources are yet to be developed and applied. The lumberers are a race of men peculiar to Canada, Maine, and New Brunswick. In the depth of winter their work in the backwoods begins. It is then they set forth to fell the huge white and red pines, which are drawn out of the snow by oxen and piled on or by the side of the frozen rivers, till the return of spring gives them an opportunity of floating them down in rafts and masses which fill all the surface of the streams in May for miles and miles. By hauling the pine logs over cliffs and dragging them down ravines the lumberers before the thaw sets in manage to collect along the banks of the various tributaries of the Ottawa and St. Lawrence some millions of cubic feet of timber, and when the ice-bound streams are free once more, their more arduous and dangerous labour recommences. Loosely joined together in huge, rough, uncouth rafts, the logs are set adrift, and with a few poles and misshapen oars to guide them, the lumberer goes in charge down currents and rapids of deep rivers, swollen and flowing fiercely with the waters from the melting snow. As long as the logs hold together all is well, but hurried and tumbled over rapids they often break up, and woe betide the unhappy lumberers who are on them when the great logs come rolling in fierce confusion one over the other, and go smashing down the rapids from rock to rock till they are all cast adrift in some open reach. When such accidents occur, as they do frequently, it sometimes happens that the logs get so wedged and bound together on the brow of some strong rapid that they remain immovable, and all the miles of logs which are following them are stopped at once. It then becomes necessary to cut the obstructing logs or "timber jam," as it is called, with axes. Only the bravest, coolest, and most experienced of the lumberers can attempt this most dangerous of all their tasks, for when once the logs which bar the passage are half cut through the might of the press behind breaks them like straws, and some 10,000 trunks of trees come plunging down with a rush and confusion that but too often renders all the coolness and activity of those who are trying to escape the avalanche of no avail.

Taking the steamer "Queen Victoria" at Grenville, which is always waiting, on the arrival of the train, the route lies through a densely wooded country, in many places in as primitive a state as when the Jesuit missionaries first sailed up this river; the current is gentle, and the scenery is diversified by numerous islands, the foliage of whose trees seems almost to touch the water, and by the glimpses which are obtained of the infant settlements upon the skirts of the forest and the margin of the stream. Six miles from Grenville the steamer touches at the small town of L'Orignal, on the Upper Canada side. This is the stopping place for those who wish to visit CALEDONIA SPRINGS, nine miles distant. The medicinal qualities of these springs (the "Plantagenet Water" of commerce) have of late years attracted considerable attention, especially among those who are troubled with rheumatic or cutaneous affections. It is said the medicinal properties of these springs were first discovered by pigeons flocking in large quantities to them; and the well known *penchant* of that bird for any salt substance led to an investigation, which resulted in the waters being brought into notice. The "season" here, which may be styled the Canadian Harrowgate, is during the heats of August; and to the invalid seeking a quiet locality, with agreeable society, this place will afford both. Nothing further of note occurs till we pass Thurso, a flourishing village, doing a large business in lumber, and Buckingham, near the junction of the River du Lièvre. The latter is a village of about 2,000 inhabitants, five miles from the Ottawa River, mostly connected with the lumber trade, a very large quantity being floated down the river which runs through the village, the mills there employing a large number of hands, and turning out about 40,000,000 feet per annum. Buckingham, within twenty miles of Ottawa, is a very picturesque village, there being in it two waterfalls, called the Upper and Lower Fall, the former about forty feet in height, though, from its incline, being so broken, it assumes more the form of a rapid; the latter has a height of about seventy feet, and falls into a basin so hemmed in that it creates a perfect whirlpool before its waters can find an outlet to the channel about ten feet below. The timber as soon as it leaves the mills is conveyed through slides (the river being unnavigable from rapids) four miles to "the basin," where it is made up into rafts and floated to its market. The River du Lièvre is a very beautiful river and well worthy of a visit. Good accommodation can be had at McKnight's private hotel, whence the tourist can start by vehicle for the High Falls, some twenty-five miles up the river, or else take a canoe (which is by far the most preferable method of travelling, in consequence of the bad roads) and so combine journeying through pleasant river scenery, and trolling at the same time, as the river abounds with pike and an occasional large trout, which readily take a spoon. These High Falls are a magnificent clear fall or *chute* of water over a precipice of about 150 feet in height, and in the spring, when the water of the river is high from the melting of the snow, present a magnificent appearance. From their distance from the settlements and difficulty of access, these falls are comparatively unknown; but as the Government employés at Ottawa will probably be on the look-out for summer resorts, this locality cannot long remain unvisited. The falls in their appearance very much resemble Montmorenci, though having more of the Horse-shoe form. Still further on is White Fish Lake, a great resort for fishermen, but most unceremoniously given up to the torch and the spear in the fall; it being no unusual thing for residents of Buckingham to spear there in two or three days one or even two barrels of large fish. The scenery on this lake is very beautiful, and a remarkable cave exists there called "the Church;" the roof of it is dome-shaped, and at the extremity of the cave is a curious raised mass of stone, called the "altar," from its strange resemblance to such; the floor is strewed with beautiful fine white sand; and as the entrance to it is very small, it is used frequently by hunters as a camping place. Probably if it could speak it could reveal tales of Indian warfare and stratagem. In the lake is an island very rich in metallic ore; in fact the whole range of mountains which traverse these backwoods teems with mineral wealth. About five miles north-east from Buckingham, and between it and Thurso, lie some newly worked plumbago or black-lead mines, which are very prolific; and antimony is said to have been discovered at Lake Donaldson, a few miles distant.

One mile below Ottawa City the River Gatineau, which has a course of 350 miles, and is the largest and most important tributary of the Ottawa River, joins it. Seven miles up occur the "Farmer's Rapids and Falls," and for the next three and a half miles, four or five rapids and cascades occur, presenting to view a most picturesque portion of this extraordinary river. On this river, forty miles up, is Lake St. Mary's,—Pemachunga—and "Thirty-one-mile-long Lake"—all splendid fishing places, but deep in the solitude of the forest, no settlements being near them.

About 6 p.m. the "Queen Victoria" arrives at her wharf at Ottawa, and as this city has received the notoriety of being the Capital of Canada, as well as from the beautiful scenery in its vicinity, the traveller will probably remain here some little time, and we will endeavour to give a short description of the city and its surroundings. OTTAWA, or as it was originally called, BYTOWN, 126 miles from Montreal, was laid out under the command of Col. By, of the Royal Engineers, who constructed the Rideau Canal, and forms three districts, viz.: *Lower Town* on the east; *Central Town* on the west, and *Upper Town* on the north-west. All of them, however, are on the south-west side of the Ottawa River, and so in Canada West. The streets are all wide and regularly laid out, and it reflects great credit on the engineering skill employed. Most of the buildings in the town are exceedingly plain, but substantially built, and being of grey limestone, much resemble in appearance some of the streets of Montreal. From Barrack Hill, the highest elevation of the town, the view is one of surpassing grandeur and extent, combining in it a trinity of river, landscape, and water-fall scenery, which few places can boast of. In the North-West, towards Chelsea, is a range of hills, one of which is conspicuous as towering above the others, and remarkable for its naked summit, locally called "Bald Mountain," looming up in the distance, all of which add to the beauty of the scene. Here many of the names seem associated with Quebec, for instance, the Chaudière Falls, and the divisions into Upper and Lower Town—probably from the intimate connection between the two cities, induced by the lumber trade, these affinities of names have sprung. Barrack Hill is in many respects a counterpart of the citadel of Quebec; in the rear is Central Town, whilst Upper and Lower Town are completely commanded by it on each side; in front is a precipitous embankment, running down almost perpendicularly to the river, thus completely sweeping it and the opposite shore north, south, and east. From this Ottawa may be said to occupy one of the finest natural positions, and in that respect is the key to an immense territory of back country, valuable in wood and minerals. This hill, the site of the Government buildings, rises almost perpendicularly from the river about 250 feet, and the group of the buildings forms a most picturesque object from every approach to the city. The structure, consisting of the Parliament and Departmental Buildings, forms three sides of a large square, facing the city, and from its position it overlooks most of the houses. The whole is in the Italian Gothic style, and built of a stone found in the vicinity, two colors being used, a warm tint set off with

Barrack Hill and new Parliament Buildings, Ottawa, C. W.

NOTMAN, Photo.

lighter dressings, which gives a rich and ornate appearance, and the stones being undressed reflect the light and give a sparkling effect in the sun. The Parliament Building is about 475 feet in length, the body of it 40 feet high, with slanting roofs. The Legislative Halls, one on each side of the interior court, are as large as those of the British Parliament, being 90 feet long and 45 feet in breadth. The library is capable of holding 300,000 volumes. The principal tower is not yet at its full height of 180 feet. The grounds in front will be laid out in terraces, with lawns, fountains, &c.; and when completed the beauty of the situation and elegance of the buildings, will enable the capital to compare with any in the world.

Besides the Parliament Buildings, several of the Departmental Offices, such as the Queen's Printing House, and numerous churches, among which the Roman Catholic Church may be mentioned as one of the handsomest in Canada, add greatly to the stable appearance of the city.

Ottawa is connected with Lake Ontario by means of the Rideau Canal, the entrance of which is at Kingston, ninety-five miles distant. It was originally constructed by the Imperial Government for military purposes, and has in it forty-seven locks, but it is now the outlet for a great amount of the local traffic. This means of communication is more correctly a succession of raised waters by means of dams, with natural lakes intervening, than a canal, properly speaking. Lake Rideau is the summit pond, and the waters which burst out at the White Fish Falls flow into the Gananoque River, which is the waste-weir for regulating the water in Lake Rideau. Thus the water in the whole canal, whether in times of flood or drought, is kept at a steady height. In Ottawa eight magnificent stone locks empty the canal into the river, and a massive cut stone bridge crosses it. At the western extremity of the city are the Chaudière Falls, a scene of imposing grandeur and beauty, and in the opinion of many second only to the Falls of Niagara. They are forty feet in height and over two hundred in width, they are situated near the centre of the river, and the waters that flow over them are strongly compressed by rocks that stretch out and impede them. In the great Chaudière (or Caldron) the sounding line has not found bottom at 300 feet. It is supposed that similarly as at Niagara, there are subterranean currents, which convey the immense mass of waters beneath the river. In fact half a mile lower down it comes boiling up again from *the Kettles*, which never freezes in the coldest weather. Immediately below the falls the river is spanned by an elegant and durable suspension bridge, which connects Upper and Lower Canada, and from which a splendid view of the foaming chasm is obtained. At the north-east end of the city, are two other falls, over which the waters of the Rideau River pour themselves with wild impetuosity into the bosom of the Ottawa; and although inferior to the Chaudière in point of sublimity and grandeur, they are not without many attractions to the admirer of Nature's works. Altogether the scenery round the city is of unsurpassed beauty—wild, romantic, and picturesque, presenting a variety rarely to be met with in any other part of the Province. The commerce of Ottawa is constituted almost wholly of lumber, both square and sawn, which passes through the city from the forests in the rear. At this point are the great timber slides, invented by the late Ruggles Wright, Esq., of which we append the following description:

When a quantity of lumber is brought down to the falls, a special contrivance called a "slide" or "shoot" is necessary to get it past them, as the result of getting it over the falls themselves would be simply to destroy the logs. For this purpose then, a certain portion of the river is dammed off, and turned into a broad wide channel of timber, and down which artificial but most rapid of all rapids in America the waters of the Ottawa rush at terrific speed. The head of this slide is placed some 300 yards above the falls, and terminates after a run of about three-quarters of a mile, in the still waters of the river below. As, however, a raft on such a steep incline, and hurried along by such a mass of water, would attain a speed which would destroy itself and all upon it, the fall of the shoot is broken at intervals by straight runs, along which it glides at comparatively reduced speed, till it again drops over, and commences another headlong rush. Some of these runs terminate with a perpendicular drop of some four or five feet, over which the raft goes headlong and wallows in the boiling water beneath, till the current again gets the mastery, and forces it on faster and more furiously than before. More than 20,000,000 cubic feet of timber come down the shoots of the Ottawa in this manner each year. The rafts are generally made of from fifteen to twenty trees, with two transverse ones to secure them at each end, and a kind of raised bridge for the lumberers to stand upon, who without such aid would be washed off it, as the mass drops from shoot to shoot down these rapids and disappears some few feet under water each plunge.

To go down the rapids of the St. Lawrence is comparatively nothing; but to go down the rapids of a timber shoot, to keep pace with the flying waters, and to see them hissing and rushing up over the raft beneath your feet, is the most exhilarating adventure in all the répertoire of American travels. It is something which partakes of flying and swimming; the immense speed of the whole mass,—the rush of the water,—the succession of shoots stretching out before you like sloping steps of stairs,—the delight of flying over these with the easy skim of a bird,—the rough long straights in which the raft seems to dive and founder, letting the water up beneath, and over it behind, till it is again urged forward; and then comes another incline of water, which you whirl madly down as if you were in a swing. To steady yourself on the narrow plank amidships, and hold on with might and main as the timber snaps and groans and works like a bundle of reeds, getting a momentary rest with each incline, and again thumping over the straights, with sharp uneasy struggles, is to experience such sensations as neither balloon nor diving bells afford, such a whirl as only three-quarters of a mile down the great timber shoots of the Ottawa can ever give. We would recommend all travellers desirous of novelty, by all means to make one of these trips, which can easily be done by making application to any of the large lumbering establishments, and judiciously disposing a trifling "backsheesh" among the voyageurs themselves.

It will be easily seen that with such a manageable motor, with navigation at its foot, both from Lake Ontario and the River St. Lawrence, Ottawa is, as it ought to be, the emporium of the truly Canadian staple—lumber—and the supply furnished here, is the main dependence of the spring and fall fleets of shipping which arrive in this country, for return cargoes to Europe, as also to a large extent for the market of the United States, in which the demand is constantly increasing. The Hull Iron Mines, distant from the city about seven miles, on the Lower Canada side, promise to be a source of considerable wealth; and in the event of the Ottawa Ship Canal being carried into effect, Ottawa will stand on the great water highway to the West. By it a navigable communication, far removed from the frontier, will be opened between Montreal and Lake Huron. Even as a military work, this would be important, as by means of it gunboats could be taken to the Upper Lakes in the event of war. The distance between Liverpool and Chicago would be shortened 760 miles more than by the Erie Canal and New York as its outlet; and the Western and North-Western States would be brought into a greater union of common interests. There is very good partridge-shooting all around in the neighbourhood, and ten or twelve miles back bears and deer are numerous.

The hotels are well kept, and moderate in their charges, and for healthiness in the summer few cities can boast its equal. Its only drawback is the want of water works, which, however, will doubtless soon be supplied.

The following account of the founding of Ottawa or Bytown is related as a fact :—About the close of the last century, a Mr. Wright, of Boston, having obtained a grant of a large tract of land upon both sides of the river, below the Chaudière Falls, and deciding that the south-side was unfit for settlement, fixed upon what is now called Hull, as the site of a village, which, from the pine lumber floated by him down to Quebec and Montreal, soon became the nucleus of a lumbering population. As cash was scarce, wages were then paid in either goods, rum, or land. In course of time, having to settle with his teamster, named Sparks, for some $200 due to him, he prevailed on him, after much grumbling, to take the hills on the southern side (now Ottawa) in payment, throwing in, in the bargain, a yoke of oxen. Years afterwards, the Canadian authorities wishing to find a channel in the interior for the conveyance of the munitions of war to the Upper Lakes, as the St. Lawrence was too much exposed to the assaults of the Americans, inaugurated the scheme of the Rideau Canal. Mr Sparks, one day in 1823, was much surprised at seeing a crowd of engineer officers and soldiers advancing to these sandy bluffs, and taking possession of them as the Ordnance property of the British Crown, under an officer named By ; the work progressed, and as the necessary shops and shanties were erected on either side the hills, they were called by way of joke upper and lower town ; finally, a bridge was thrown across the Fall connecting Hull or Wrightstown with Bytown, and as the latter slowly grew, the other remained stationary. Money flowed in on Mr. Sparks ; he sold lots, and was eventually reputed worth half a million of dollars, and the long despised hills eventually were decided upon by the Queen to sustain the Parliament

Buildings of United Canada. Sparks Street, named after the founder, is now one of the principal streets of Ottawa.

One mile and a half above Ottawa we come to the "Little Chaudière Falls," a pretty fall of thirteen feet, and two miles above that the rapid known under the name of "The Remoux," between which and the Little Chaudière the river expands into wide lake-like basins. Four and a half miles above this are the De Cheine rapids, opposite the Village of Britannia, formed by a ridge of limestone crossing the course of the river, and having a fall of about nine feet. Above this, nine miles from Ottawa, on the Lower Canada side, is Aylmer, situated on a splendid open reach of the river, twenty-six miles in length, called *Lac de Cheine*, and navigable for vessels of the largest class. Proceeding onwards we come to the celebrated CHATS PORTAGE or CHATS FALLS, which are a series of cascades, of about twenty feet high, extending for about three miles, broken by islands, along the edge of which the steamer runs, covered with hemlock, cedar, pine, many of them unvisited by man, with about a dozen deep channels, presenting a most remarkable appearance, not unlike the Lake of the Thousand Islands in miniature. At one point no less than thirteen falls are visible at once. A tramway of four miles in length connects the navigable reaches above and below. An attempt was made by the Provincial Government to construct a canal for the purpose of overcoming these falls and rapids, which have an aggregate height of fifty feet; but after nearly all the excavation was complete, and a large portion of the stone for the lock prepared, the work was suspended in 1857, and is now lying unprofitable and useless, leaving a monument of ill-directed efforts, painful to contemplate. Above the rapids the magnificent LAKE DES CHATS, is about twenty miles long and one mile wide, though its spacious bays extend it to three miles. On the south shore is Kinnel Lodge, near ARNPRIOR, at the confluence of the Madawaska and Ottawa

Rivers, belonging to the Highland Chief McNab, who first settled this portion of the Upper Ottawa, about the year 1824, but it was not regularly laid out till 1851, when the property came into the hands of D. McLachlan, Esq., who had the honor of entertaining the Prince of Wales, while on his tour on the Ottawa. Here His Royal Highness planted a young oak in memorial of his visit, which may be seen by the tourist. Arnprior is forty miles from Ottawa City, and a station on the Ottawa & Brockville Railway, whence the tourist may take the cars on his return trip to Montreal; but while up here we would recommend him by all means to proceed about twenty miles further to PORTAGE DU FORT, where several islands divide the river into a number of channels, and it is crossed by a reef of crystalized limestone, forming the *Portage du Fort Rapids*, or more properly speaking, Falls. At the head of the largest island is situated the village, named after the rapids, on the Canada side, which is one of the principal business places for lumbermen. The whole distance lies through magnificent scenery: river, lake, plain, rapid, and mountain succeed each other, and form a fairy landscape of varied interest and beauty. Nature has been no niggard of her benefits to this section of the Ottawa Valley. The soil is rich in production, and the hills abound in minerals. This is the belt of country where the change from the gneiss and primitive to the metamorphic limestone rock occurs, and it is at such points that these productions are to be with certainty looked for. For some distance the banks of the river are composed of white marble. Between Portage du Fort Village and the head of the *Calumet Falls*, a distance of seven miles, by a good macadamized road, the tourist reaches the next navigable point of the Ottawa, which is open to the Chapeau Rapids, on the north side of Alumette Island, opposite to, but five miles from Pembroke, on the south, or by the south channel and Westmeath to

Hawley's Island, two and a half miles below the latter town. In addition to the scenery, one object of historical interest presents itself, respecting which we quote Dr. Taché :—"In ascending the great River Ottawa, one has to stop at the rock of the high mountain, situate in the middle of the portage of the seven *chutes*, at the foot of the island of the *Grand Calumet*. It is here lies Cadieux's tomb, surrounded to this day by a wooden railing. Each time the Company's (Hudson Bay) canoes pass the little rock an old voyageur relates to his younger companions the fate of the brave interpreter." His history is somewhat as follows :—Cadieux was a roving interpreter, who had married a young Algonquin girl, and purchased at this portage furs for the traders. After a winter thus passed he ascertained that a party of Iroquois were waiting to pounce on the canoes. To prevent this, he and a young brave endeavoured to inveigle the Iroquois into the woods, while the canoes descended the rapids, and by a circuitous route himself rejoin the voyageurs. He succeeded in the first part of his design ; but when thirteen days had elapsed, and Cadieux had not been heard from, a party was sent to scour the woods, who found a small hut of boughs, and the corpse of the interpreter half covered with green branches. His hands were clasped over a large sheet of birch bark, on which was scribbled his tale of exhaustion, hunger and death. The piece of bark on which his death song was written (for Cadieux was a poet) was brought to the post of the Lake of the Two Mountains, and the voyageurs of to-day have set it to a plaintive melody, which is much in the style of the old Norman ballads.

At Pembroke, seventy miles from Ottawa, the last link of the steamboat navigation of the Ottawa commences, ending at Des Joachim, forty miles higher up the stream, passing through the Upper and Lower Alumette Lakes with all their soft and romantic beauties, and through the stern and gloomy grandeur of the Deep River, whose mountains of 600 feet in height rise from the water's edge, the depths of which are little less in profundity.

Des Joachim, the last of steamboat navigation, is fifty miles from the mouth of the River Matawan, the connecting stream between the Ottawa and Lake Nipissing, through which the proposed Ottawa and Lake Huron navigation is destined to run. Above the Falls and Portage "*des Alumettes*," one hundred miles up the river from Ottawa, there are few or no settlements; and the shanty of the lumberman or the hunter are the only marks of civilization that break the monotony of the forest. The lakes which abound throughout this back country are not only too numerous to mention, but their names in the Indian language are almost unpronounceable.

Returning down the river, where splendid pike fishing is to be had, and an occasional salmon-trout, the tourist will meet the train either at Sandpoint, the terminus of the Brockville Railroad (a pretty little village), or proceed five miles further to Arnprior, whence the cars start daily for Brockville. BROCKVILLE is one of the pleasantest villages in the Province, situated on an elevation of land which rises from the river in a succession of ridges; the houses are built with considerable taste, and joined with the terrace-like formation of land, it has an appearance of elegance and ease not often met with in Canada. It contains about 5000 inhabitants, and, being the junction of the Ottawa Railway and Grand Trunk, has a good deal of local traffic; it was named after General Brock; it is a good stopping-place for sportsmen, being at the foot of the Lake of the Thousand Islands, and so affording accommodation to those who are attracted to this spot either for shooting or for scenery. A small sheet of water, Charleston Lake, lies 17 miles back, whose scenery is lovely. Fish abound in it, and it is not unusual for the sportsman to take one hundred bass with a single line in one day. The boating on it in summer is excellent; the shore is lined with boat-houses, and there are several handsome steam and sail yachts on it. A ferry-boat plies every half-hour between Brockville and Morrisburg, in New York State, almost opposite, two or three miles from which is a spot where a view of one hundred islands can be gained at one time.

Leaving Brockville by the evening train for Kingston, 47 miles distant, we arrive there at midnight; and this being the point where we purpose taking steamer to come down the St. Lawrence and enjoy the scenery of the "Thousand Islands," Rapids, &c., it is as well to take a day or two to see the city and its environs.

KINGSTON, called by the Indians "*Cataraqui*," was the original capital of Upper Canada. A settlement was begun here by the French, under De Courcelles, as early as 1672, under the name of Fort Cataraqui, and the fort subsequently received the name of Fort Frontenac, in honor of the French Count of that name. This fort was afterwards in the possession of the French and the Indians, until it was destroyed by the expedition under Colonel Bradstreet in 1758. In 1762 the place fell into the hands of the British, from whom it received its present name. The advantageous position of this city, from being at the outlet of Lake Ontario into the St. Lawrence, and at the junction of the waters of the Bay of Quinte and the great Cataraqui Creek, together with the Rideau Canal, has made it a place of considerable commercial importance. As a military station, its defences are only second to Quebec. About half-a-mile to the east is a low peninsula, ending in Point Frederick, which, with the other parallel one terminating in Point Henry, encloses Navy Bay, the depot for the maritime armament of Britain on the lakes during the war of 1812. On an eminence of the peninsula is Fort Henry, commanding the entrance to the lake: this, together with large substantial martello towers, has complete command of the harbour. Point Frederick is connected with the town by a wooden-bridge, 600 yards in length, across Cataraqui Bay. It is solidly constructed, and near it are the the Marine Barracks. The harbour of Kingston is formed by Wolfe and Garden Islands lying across the bay, three miles distant : this is a beautiful sheet of water, and a commodious safe refuge for ships of the largest class. Ship and boat-building is carried on at Kingston to a great extent, and vessels for both lake and ocean navigation are built and fitted out complete.

About a mile to the west of the city lies the Provincial Penitentiary, a large and massive stone building, surrounded by a high and most substantial wall, with towers at the corners. The arrangements are so complete that escape for the convicts, under any circumstances, seems impossible. The cells are so arranged that each keeper has a great number of prisoners, apart from each other, completely under his eye in his rounds, and can, at all times, ascertain without being perceived what is going on. The different trades all find employment in different workshops, and those who enter without a trade are immediately put to learn one. The silent system is pursued except in necessary intercommunication at work. The whole arrangements are conducted upon the principle of the U. S. State prisons ; and to those who have never been through a place of convict confinement, we would by all means recommend a visit. Near the Penitentiary are baths and mineral springs, which have been of late years and are still much frequented. The public buildings of the city are very fine, the principal of which is the Market House, so-called, above which is the Town Hall, and from the dome surmounting it a very extensive view is obtained. Here, also, are two colleges—Queen's and Regiopolis, both conspicuous structures.

Leaving Kingston by one of the steamers from the West, early in the morning, the tourist will get one of the finest views to be met with in Canada, and one which, like Niagara, though often described in various ways, is really *indescribable* to do it justice,—The Lake of the Thousand Islands.

The river issuing from the eastern extremity of Lake Ontario is now, for the first time, called the St. Lawrence. This name was given to the mighty river by Jacques Cartier, who began to explore it on the festival of that martyr. In the course of a few miles the channel becomes so wide, and so full of islands, that it has obtained the name of "THE LAKE OF THE THOUSAND ISLANDS." These islands, which have obtained a world-wide celebrity, consist of fully 1800 in number, of every imaginable shape, size, and appearance, some of them barely visible, others covering many acres; some only a few yards long, others several miles in length; some presenting little or nothing but bare masses of rock, whilst others are so thickly wooded over, that nothing but the most gorgeous green foliage in summer is to be seen, whilst in autumn, the leaves present colours of different hues of light crimson, yellow, purple and other colours scarcely imaginable. They are truly "emerald gems in the ring of the wave," and their broken outline presents the most picturesque combinations of wood and water. The first or largest of these islands is Grand or Wolfe Island, containing about 9,000 acres, to which there is a ferry-boat constantly plying from Kingston; it is of an irregular shape, and indented by numerous bays. Betwixt its western shore and the city of Kingston lies Garden Island, containing about 30 acres, belonging to a firm largely engaged in the rafting business. They employ a large number of vessels in bringing staves from the western portion of the Upper Province to the island, where they are made into rafts for the voyage to Quebec. The boundary line between the United States and the British dominions extends along the middle of the south channel of the St. Lawrence, passing by Cape Vincent on the American shore (a pretty little village), the terminus of the Watertown and Cape Vincent Railroad, and afterwards passes between "Duck Island" and the "Galops Islands." Westward, though scarcely one of the thousand islands, lies Amherst Island, the original French name of which was the "Isle of Tanti": it now belongs to the Earl of Mountcashel; 5,000 acres of it are under good cultivation. The channels between the extremities and the mainland are called the Upper and Lower Gaps. As a fishing ground for pike, maskinongé, black bass, doré, &c., no part of the St. Lawrence can compare with the shores of these islands. The largest-sized maskinongé are taken here, not with an ordinary bait, for they scorn the small bait that is so tempting a morsel to their kindred pike; "but," says Weld, a good fishing authority, speaking of this locality, "I have invariably taken them with fish of a large size, such as no other angler would ever think of putting on his line." Forty or fifty pounds is not an unusual weight for them, and instances are not wanting where much larger ones have been caught. Lanman, in his "Wanderings," makes mention of a maskinongé he took here which weighed 49 lbs., was nearly 8 feet in length, and took one hour and a quarter to land after he was first hooked. (Vide "Small's Fresh-water Fish," p. 45.) There is also very good spearing here at night, and a week or two spent on either of these islands will amply repay the fisherman, besides giving him the invigorating benefits resulting from the lake breeze. There is no difficulty in getting canoes or accommodations at any of the farm-houses, but hotels are few and far between. The whole channel of the Lake of the Thousand Islands is a famous spot for sporting; myriads of wild fowls of every description may be found here, and the facilities for coming upon them round some interposing point, by suddenly rounding one of the many islets, or, again, by lying concealed on one of the islets and taking them on the wing in their flight past, make this amusement more varied than in most other shooting grounds. It is necessary to have a good Newfoundland dog or retriever when shooting from the shore. These islands, too, have been the scene of thrilling romance. From their great number and labyrinth-like channels among them, they afforded an admirable retreat for the insurgents in the last Canadian insurrection, as well as for the American sympathizers with them, who, under the questionable name of *patriots*, sought only to embarrass the British Government. In 1838, a band of men, headed by one Johnson, took refuge among these islands, setting all authorities at defiance, and provided with boats of surprising lightness, they committed the most audacious outrages both up and down the river, and baffled all pursuit. The story is told of them, when he was obliged, from close pursuit, to separate from his band, his daughter, with a devotedness and courage that was inimitable, supplied him herself with the necessaries of life in these solitary retreats, and rowed him in her canoe from one island to another under cover of night.

The passage through the "Thousand Islands" by steamer is generally made in the early morning, leaving Kingston about daylight. You pass close to, and near enough often to cast a pebble from the deck of the steamer on to them, cluster after cluster of circular little islands, whose trees, perpetually moistened by the water, have a most luxuriant leaf, their branches overhanging the current. Again, you pass little winding passages and bays between the islands, the trees on their margins interlacing above them, and forming here and there natural bowers; yet the waters of these bays are so deep that steamers might pass under their shade. Then opens up a magnificent sheet of water, many miles wide, with a large island apparently dividing it into two great rivers; but as you approach it, you discover that it is but a group of small islands, the river being divided into many parts, looking like silver threads. Again, the river seems to come to an abrupt termination four or five hundred yards in advance of you, but as you approach the threatening rocks, a channel suddenly opens out on the right, you are whirled suddenly into it, and the next moment a magnificent amphitheatre of lake opens out before you. This, again, to all appearance, is bounded by a dense green bank, but at your approach the mass is moved, as if in a kaleidoscope, and a hundred beautiful little isles appear in its place. Such, for upwards of forty miles, is the scenery through which you glide. Once seen, the remembrance of them is never forgotten; and when seen under the bright rays of an early summer dawn, it seems a glimpse of fairy land. Emerging from this beautiful scenery, we come suddenly upon Brockville (before mentioned), and, proceeding onwards, nothing further of note occurs till we come to PRESCOTT, 12 miles down the St. Lawrence, which is a very thriving town. This is the terminus of the Ottawa and Prescott Railroad, a road doing a large business, as Prescott, being opposite to Ogdensburgh, in New York State, and connected with it by means of two ferry-boats, is the place of transhipment for most of the American goods purchased by the dwellers on the Ottawa, as well as for the export of cattle and Canadian produce. This road was built for the purpose of counteracting the stagnation of trade resulting from the construction of the Rideau Canal between Kingston and Ottawa, which diverted the carrying trade previously enjoyed by Prescott; and this shows how one enterprise stimulates another. The view from the town is exceedingly picturesque, embracing the villa residences, spires, lighthouse, and miniature docks of Ogdensburgh; and as all passing steamers call at the one place or the other during the summer, while in the winter a passage is kept open by the heavy railroad steamer, it wears continually an aspect of stir and business. The country around is very pleasant and healthy. Fort Wellington here is a military position of importance, and forms an object of considerable attraction. About a mile below Prescott are the ruins of an old stone windmill, at a place called *Windmill Point*, in which, as well as an adjoining stone house, in 1838 (the second insurrection), a body of Americans, numbering about 400, who had sailed from the vicinity of Sackett's harbour under Von Shultz, a Polish exile, and landed at Prescott, took refuge when attacked by Colonel Young; here they defended themselves bravely, and killed eighteen of the British. The walls were too strong to be reduced without cannon, and some guns and additional troops were brought up. An attack was then made, when the party in the mill tried to escape, but 156 were taken prisoners and sent to Kingston for trial. Two miles east is the quaint old town of Johnstown, formerly the county town of Leeds and Grenville. At Spencerville, a small village eight miles distant, the sportsman may find plenty of deer. About five miles below Prescott is Chimney Island, on which are to be seen the remains of an old French fortification. At this island is the first rapid on the river. Opposite to Prescott is OGDENSBURGH, on the American shore, at the mouth of the Osgewatchie, on its west bank. This is a place of some importance, a railway to Rouse's Point connecting it with Boston and Montreal. The remains of the original fort called "La Presentation," and built in 1748, are still to be seen. Twenty-one miles further on we pass Morrisburg, at the foot of the *Rapide de Plat*, a thriving town, a short distance below which lies *Chrysler's Farm*, where, in 1813, a battle was fought between the English and the Americans. The former were commanded by General Morrison with 800 men; the latter, who were the *élite* of the army, under Gen. Boyd, were defeated with great slaughter, forced to retire to their boats, and ultimately reached Plattsburg. Thirty miles below Ogdensburgh is Louisville, whence stages run to MASSENA SPRINGS, seven miles distant. These springs are five in number, on the banks of the River Racket. The largest is called St. Regis Spring, in honour of the tribe of Indians of that name who discovered its virtues, and long ago used its medicinal waters. Massena is a place of popular resort among the northern New Yorkers and Vermonters, and of late years numbers of Canadians have visited the springs: and from their beautiful surroundings and vicinity to the Long Sault Rapids, only four or five miles distant, they are a very pleasant summer watering-place. The United States Hotel is a large first-class house, where may be had good horses and carriages, boats and fishing tackle. Visitors coming from Montreal can take the Montreal steamers to Louisville Landing, and by stage, or *via* Rouse's Point and Potsdam Junction. Proceeding onwards we come to DICKINSON'S LANDING, 77 miles from Montreal, a station on the Grand Trunk, and lying at the head of the Cornwall Canal and the Long Sault Rapids. These rapids are nine miles in length, divided in the centre by several islands in a continuous line. Both the north and south channel can be used, but the south is generally preferred; the velocity of the current here is exceedingly swift, a raft drifting through in forty minutes. The Cornwall Canal, built to avoid these rapids, is the longest of all the St. Lawrence canals, being 11½ miles: it is only needed for vessels bound up the river, as from the size and regular inclination of the rapids steamers and other vessels have no difficulty in descending the river. The scenery of the Long Sault Rapids is excitingly beautiful; here and there the surging waters present all the appearance of the ocean in a storm, in other places their surface is perfectly unruffled,—a deceptive stillness from their very velocity; and the raft that meets the eye in its passage over, apparently doomed to destruction, swiftly rounds some threatening obstacle, leaving it far in its wake. Great strength, dexterity, and courage, are required and employed in passing them. The voyageurs who man the rafts are a peculiar class, and a slight description of them will not be amiss here. Gay and mirthful by nature and habit, patient and enduring at labour, seeking neither ease nor wealth—they let the morrow take care of itself. When enduring the severest hardships they will joke and laugh, and sing their Canadian songs, the majority of which are extemporaneous, and of a rude character.

At the lower end of the Long Sault Rapids, the two currents of the north and south channels meet and dash against each other with great impetuosity, forming what is called the "Big Pitch." This is almost directly opposite the pleasant and stirring town of CORNWALL, sixty-eight miles from Montreal, which, though very lively from the constant transit of steamers, &c., through the canal, has little other trade than that of being the county town. Excellent duck-shooting is to be had in the fall of the year here, the birds staying at the foot of the rapids for several weeks on their passage southwards ; canoes can always be had in the town with an Indian attendant, who, with a good sportsman, will thoroughly enter into the excitement of the sport, and guide him to the favourite resorts of the teal, the mallard, and widgeon. Nearly opposite to Cornwall, situated partly in the United States and partly in Canada, for the boundary line of 45° strikes the St. Lawrence there, is the Indian village of St. Regis. Here, on a small portion of the hunting-grounds of their once powerful nation, a settlement of Iroquois exists. The number of British and American Indians is about 900. Many of the men continue to procure a precarious subsistence by hunting, and the women employ themselves in making up the skins of animals killed in winter into mitts and moccasins, and in manufacturing splint baskets and brooms. There is a large stone church here, with a steeple and two bells, respecting one of which is the following history :—Purchased in France by means of furs sent out by themselves, it was captured by an English cruiser, taken to Salem, Mass., and afterwards purchased for the church at Deerfield. Their priest, hearing of this, excited them to a crusade for its recovery, and they, coming suddenly on that village under cover of darkness,

The Squaw—Basket Maker—(by Kreighoff).

Notman, Photo.

slew and took prisoners all the inhabitants; then, fastening the bell to a long pole, it was carried on their shoulders 150 miles, and buried in the woods near what is now Burlington, Vermont, whence, in the following spring, it was safely conveyed to the belfry built for its original reception. After passing St. Regis, the St. Lawrence flows unrestrictedly through British dominions. At a little distance below Cornwall the river expands into a lake, five and a half miles in width, and twenty-five miles long, called Lake St. Francis. The surface of this lake, especially near the foot of it, is interspersed with a great number of small islands, which add to the beauty of the expanse of waters;—it is a noticeable fact that at the foot of almost all the rapids, the river widens considerably, as if to show by contrast how smooth and placid its waters might be, after their wild and tumultuous course in the narrow passes. Passing the village of *Lancaster*, on the north shore of the lake, about midway, we come to COTEAU DU LAC, 30 miles from Cornwall, at the mouth of the River Delisle; this is a small village, and the name as well as style of the buildings denote its French origin. Being, however, at the head of the Coteau Rapids, it is a very pretty stopping-place, and affords excellent fishing and water-fowl shooting. Nine miles from it is the village of "CEDARS," which gives its name to a part of the rapids. In fact, the eleven miles of incline here, over which the water rushes, is divided into three sections, called, respectively, Coteau, Cedars, or Split Rock, and Cascades. The latter name probably has been given from the water falling over several ledges of rock one after the other, giving it the appearance of cascade over cascade, and causing a peculiar sensation in coming down it as the vessel glides from ledge to ledge of rock. At the foot of the Cascades on the south bank is the village of Beauharnois, 27 miles from Montreal, where vessels bound upwards enter the canal to pass round these rapids. The Beauharhois Canal is $11\frac{1}{4}$ miles long. The village is very prettily situated at the head of a bay, formed by a point of land stretching out on the west, on which is a well wooded and pretty spot called " The Grove," a favorite resort for pic-nics from Montreal. From here a fine view can be had of Montreal Mountain in the distance. Leaving Beauharnois, we find ourselves on the south side of Lake St. Louis, another expansion of the River St. Lawrence, whose north shore we sailed up on the upward journey to Ottawa city. About five miles from Beauharnois is Nun's Island, a high mound of peculiar shape, which has doubtless been an Indian post and burial-ground: it is beautifully cultivated, and belongs to the Grey Nunnery, Montreal. Near this, at the mouth of the Chateauguay River (an excellent fishing-ground), is the village of Chateauguay, one mile from which is the celebrated battle-field of Chateauguay, memorable for the victory gained there by Colonel De Salaberry, in 1813, over the American troops under General Hampton, who were repulsed with considerable loss, and obliged to fall back upon Plattsburg. Proceeding onwards we pass opposite to Lachine, ten miles from Montreal, the Indian village of CAUGHNAWAGA (pronounced Cok-na-wau-ga.) This consists of nothing but a number of Indian huts or cabins, occupied by a portion of the once powerful and ferocious tribe of the Six Nations, who subsist by navigating steamers, boats, and rafts over the rapids in summer, and in the winter by the profits arising from the sale of snow-shoes, moccasins, &c. There are about 1100 of them in number, and they are remarkable for their orderly and quiet behaviour. In early times they were distinguished for their predatory incursions upon their neighbours in the New England provinces, and the bell that now hangs in their church was the proceeds of one of these excursions. They behaved nobly during the rebellion of '37-8. While attending worship on the morning of the 4th November, '38, a party of insurgents surrounded the church; the Indians immediately turned out, and the Chief, setting an example that was promptly followed by all, raised the war whoop, seized the person next him, and wrested the musket out of his hands. The others, panic-stricken, immediately surrendered, and, tied with their own sashes, were taken prisoners to Montreal; for this act they have received special marks of Her Majesty's favour. Opposite to Caughnawaga is Lachine, whence the tourist can return to Montreal by cars, or, shooting the rapids of Lachine (before described), pass under the Victoria Bridge, and so land at the wharf in the City of Montreal.

FROM KINGSTON TO TORONTO.

Travelling westward from Kingston nothing worthy of note attracts the attention till arriving at Napanee, whence we for some time journey along the margin of the beautiful Bay of Quinte,—a bay which might with more propriety be called an estuary, it being the mode of exit of the Trent River. By means of it on the one side, and Lake Ontario on the other, is formed the peninsula of Prince Edward County. At TYENDINAGA, on the northern shore, is a settlement of the Indian tribe of Mohawks, who separated from their nation in the State of New York about 1784. They had embraced Christianity long previously, and as far back as the reign of Queen Anne were presented with a service of plate for their communion. They are Episcopalians, and their place of worship having become too small for its congregation, they built out of their own means a commodious stone edifice.

BELLEVILLE, forty-eight miles from Kingston and one hundred and twelve from Toronto, at the mouth of the River

Moira, a first-class station on the Grand Trunk, is a thriving place and well worthy of a visit. The vicinity of Belleville affords several beautiful views of the bay, one especially, about four miles below the town, where the promontory of Ox-point jutting out a long distance towards an opposite headland, Massassaga-point, on the south shore, causes the channel to contract to less than half its ordinary width. The saw-mills and piles of lumber detract considerably from the picturesque appearance of the harbour, on a near view; but the town itself presents an imposing aspect from the water, rising as it does gradually from the edge of the bay to the point of a high bluff, where the fine spire of St. Michael's Church forms a fitting apex to the view. The position of Belleville is very healthy, the heat of summer being tempered by fine westerly breezes, which prevail throughout the summer months, generally setting in about 10 a. m., and continuing to blow briskly till sunset. This may be attributable to its vicinity to Lake Ontario. This place has good communication both by rail and steam with various places of interest, the steamers that visit the port affording facilities for a trip to Picton, the Lake of the Mountain, Kingston, &c. This "LAKE OF THE MOUNTAIN" is a remarkable curiosity. About four and a half miles from Belleville, in the 2nd concession of Ameliasburgh, on the farm of D. Gibson, Esq., there exists a most perfect and unique example of a volcanic upheaval, known in the neighborhood as "The Mountain," which consists of felspar and gneiss, rising almost vertically from the plain to a height of about eighty or a hundred feet. It is about 250 yards long and half that in breadth, affording a complete exemplification of the class of natural phenomena to which it belongs. On this eminence is a remarkable, deep, and black looking lake, probably the crater of an ancient volcano; it is a favourite place of resort for pic-nic parties. The botanist will also be richly repaid in the surrounding country, which contains several rare plants. The Bay of Quinte is finely adapted for boating, either rowing or sailing, for a distance of about twelve miles to the westward and about forty miles in an easterly direction. There is very good fishing, especially for the troller; pike, bass, doré, perch, Oswego bass or sheepshead, and chub, being the principal fish. The bass and chub, which latter attain a larger size here, readily rise to the fly, and very good sport may be had with them if the day is at all cloudy. The most attractive fly in these waters seems to be an artificial bumble-bee or grasshopper. For large bass, which abound here, but are very wary, a large white moth in the dusk of the evening is a never failing bait, and the fly called the sturgeon fly seldom fails to attract. Good duck shooting may be had here on the bay, and in the marshes at Ox-point, as well as in Ameliasburgh, at the outlet of Roblin Lake. Woodcock and snipe are plentiful in the late summer and early fall, and plover abound along the shore and in the marshes. Occasionally a fox hunting party is got up with beagles, and a good run may occasionally be had, Ox-point never failing to furnish a brush. Belleville is the southern terminus of the Hastings Road, which extends north to the Madawaska River, and there will no doubt be an increased settlement along the upper part of it, as the country of the Upper Ottawa becomes more thickly populated, which it cannot fail to do if the proposed Lake Huron Canal be carried out. About twenty-six miles north of Belleville lie Belmont, Madoc, and Marmora, all of them townships rapidly rising into note from their iron mines and fine white marble quarries. This marble is of a pure whiteness, and admits of a very high polish. It is of first rate quality, and is pronounced by competent judges to be hardly if at all inferior to the celebrated Italian Carrara marble. The quarries and iron mines have both been lying in a quiescent state for some time, until recently some eminent capitalists from

Cleveland, U. S., took a large amount of stock in the united companies. They have amalgamated with the Cobourg & Peterboro' Railway, so that by boat on Rice Lake, and train from Harwood on the above mentioned road, access to the mines is made easy. The operations they intend carrying on will be on a very extensive scale, as they purpose getting out 100 to 150 tons of the ore daily, as soon as they have all their "plant" thoroughly established. Eleven miles west is TRENTON, backed by a good agricultural country, and from its position, offering great advantages of water-power; if an outlay were made in the construction of dams, machinery enough could be put in operation to supply every article of manufacture. It must eventually become a manufacturing town.

Twenty-one miles west of Belleville is the prettily laid out town of BRIGHTON, remarkable for its natural harbour of refuge, one of the best on Lake Ontario, called PRESQU' ISLE BAY. This is formed by a narrow peninsula stretching out in front of the village, forming a perfect lagoon on the east, enclosed on three sides and a half, so that whatever winds may blow, the vessels lying here are comparatively safe.

Ninety miles west of Kingston we come to COBOURG, a very busy town and prettily situated withal on the lake. It ranks only second to Toronto and Hamilton in a business point of view, from its comparative nearness to Rochester and Oswego, which are brought into daily communication with it by means of steamers. The soil around Cobourg, and in fact from here westwards, is very fertile, producing great quantities of wheat, and of a very good quality—large quantities of which find their way to Rochester, and are there mixed with American wheat, passing for Genesee flour. It is also possessed of very superior water-power, and can boast of manufactures in the shape of cloth and tweeds, which successfully compete with those of any other place for durability and quality. Here is situated Victoria College, built by the Wesleyan Methodist body, attended by about 150 students. It is a fine handsome edifice, and has a good high school in connection with it. Cobourg possesses one of the finest town halls in Canada, containing the best proportioned ball-room in the Province, and honored by the Prince of Wales on his visit. The gaol here is also a strong, massive and imposing building.

This place has the advantage of a large and well settled back country, which brings a considerable amount of business to the front; and the Cobourg & Peterboro' Railway bids fair to do a large amount of business in bringing out lumber, which is largely manufactured on the Otonabee River and connecting waters of a chain of lakes some fifteen miles north. The nearest of these to Cobourg is RICE LAKE, twelve miles distant, so called on account of the large quantities of that grain which grow there in a wild state on its banks and in its marshy edges; this the Indians gather in the fall of the year, by laying the stalks over the edges of their canoes, and then beating out the grain with a rough wooden mallet or billet of wood. This lake is nearly thirty miles long, and only seven miles wide, well studded with islands, which cause it to present a most picturesque appearance. The Otonabee River falls into it at the north from Peterborough, and the Trent River issues from its eastern extremity, falling into the Bay of Quinte, making through its irregular course a length of nearly one hundred miles. The Otonabee River connects it with a chain of lakes still further to the north; these as well as Rice Lake and the Otonabee River are but expansions and channels of the Trent itself, just as Lake St. Peter, Lake St. Francis, &c., are of the St. Lawrence. The names of the principal of these lakes in the Colborne district are *Trent, Shebauticon, Balsam, Bobcaygeon, Chemong, Pigeon, Sturgeon, Mud, Cameron,* and a host of other smaller ones. Describe one and you describe all. All of these lakes abound with fish, and to say which of them affords the best fishing ground would be a very difficult matter. We will commence with Rice Lake, in which maskinongé of the largest size have been caught, and it was only last year (1865) an American visitor from Rochester caught one that weighed upwards of 30 lbs. Black bass and perch of a large size are found. Perhaps the best fishing spot on this lake is at the mouth of the Otonabee River, on the north side, and alongside the abutments of the bridge at Harwood and Keene. There is an Indian village here, whose inhabitants are very thrifty and industrious; they belong to the tribe of the Mississaga Indians (one of the first that held Upper Canada); they are ardent lovers of the chase, and well acquainted with the best fishing and shooting places in the vicinity: on this account they are repeatedly engaged by parties who camp out in pursuit of the pleasures of the rod or gun.

At GORE's Landing, which is reached by a stage running tri-weekly, there are two comfortable inns, the only ones in the vicinity, and boats and canoes (flat-bottomed boats are the best, being less likely to upset, as well as affording more room) can be obtained from any of the residents on the lake shores, who are always glad to see the beauties of the lake appreciated by strangers, and who are very hospitable to all visitors. HARWOOD is situated at the present terminus of the Cobourg & Peterboro Railway, to which place during the summer three or four trains are intended to be regularly run daily.

In the fall of the year Rice Lake is the resort of thousands of wild ducks of every species, partridges, quail, and game birds of every description, which flock here to feed on the wild rice. As might be expected from the abundance of their food they are in excellent condition. Here may be seen the Virginia Rail in large numbers, excessively plump, and very good eating; the Bobolink having doffed his summer plumage and put on his russet coat is here as much the *rice bird* as when he reaches the swamps of Carolina a few weeks later. Bittern are numerous in the reeds, and an occasional heron may be seen standing on one leg like a statue, intent on the motions of the finny tribe, though too wary to admit of the sportsman's near approach. Snipe abound for a few weeks only, though a few remain to breed; woodcock breed here also and are numerous. There are several shooting boxes here and there along the south shore belonging to gentlemen in Cobourg, but most parties prefer camping out, being thus able to move from place to place according as the ducks, &c., are more or less plentiful. Decoys in October, when the fall ducks come in, are essential.

Proceeding up the Otonabee River, at a distance of 30 miles from Cobourg is PETERBORO', connected with it and Port Hope by rail. Till the completion of these lines it was almost cut off during the winter from communication with the front, but now all seasons of the year are alike in affording access to it. Most of its trade lies in lumber; and the various places scattered along this chain of lakes, such as Fenelon Falls, &c., situated as they are in the midst of a good pine country, intersected by numerous small streams, and with such a facility for shipment of their produce either by land or water to the lake shore, whence they mostly find their way to Oswego or Rochester, afford the greatest facilities for lumbering. FENELON FALLS village is on the Trent, between Cameron and Sturgeon Lakes, and is a very pretty picturesque spot; taking its name from a fall 20 feet high and 300 feet in width, of the horse-shoe form. A steamer from Lindsay plies daily to and fro during the summer, thus enabling the traveller to make the entire round of these lakes and return to the Trent. The town of LINDSAY is situated on Lake Scugog, and like the other places here is dependent on lumber for its principal trade, though a great deal of local traffic is done, it being the centre of a pretty well settled district. It is 40 miles from Port Hope. The tourist may go east from Fenelon Falls by steamer to Bobcaygeon, through Pigeon Lake, Buckhorn and Chemung Lakes to Bridgenorth, and if he takes canoe at the Indian village between the two latter lakes, he can go through another chain of waters which for beauty of scenery can scarcely be surpassed. LAKEFIELD, on the Otonabee River, at the south-end of *Kah-cha-wan-oo-kah Lake*, is the residence of a number of English gentlemen who have taken up their abode there chiefly on account of the attractions these back lakes afford. Strangers visiting this place meet with every civility and attention, and could never be at a loss to find abundant means of conveying themselves to the chain of beautiful lakes stretching northward half-way to the Arctic ocean. Lake Scugog, on which it is situated, is an extremely pretty sheet of water; in form it is, as it were, a double lake, being nearly divided longitudinally by a peninsula from the south; on its banks are several villages—PORT PERRY, SCUGOG, &c. The most curious feature about this lake is the large quantity of swamped timber that lines its bays; huge trees, whose lifeless branches look like spectres of the forest, stand immersed with their roots from eight to ten feet under water. This has been caused by the erection of the Government dam at Lindsay for facilitating the lumber trade, throwing the waters back and submerging the sides of the lake, especially towards its head or southern shore. But as there is no evil without some good, so these unsightly trunks and roots afford a most secure retreat for the wild fowl, which breed here undisturbed; and the largest black bass may be seen lying under the twisted roots, safe in the intricacy of the flood-wood. There is excellent night spearing on the shallows near SCUGOG village, the fish coming on to the feeding grounds at dark. The whole region on the south is woody, low and marshy; the water is clear, the bottom muddy. Trolling with a good sized bright spoon, and a thick line, never fails to secure some fine maskelongé and black bass. A short distance from Scugog village is a small island called BALD POINT ISLAND. This has been an Indian burying ground,—tradition asserts the scene of a furious contest between two hostile tribes. Great quantities of bones, teeth, pottery, and arrow heads strew the beach, and can be picked out of the clayey banks after the winter's thaw has loosened a fresh stratum of mould. It is a lovely, secluded spot, with a gravelly shore, where the water shoals gradually, making a splendid bathing ground, and save the kingfisher and occasional passing flight of the duck hawk, or the mud turtle sunning itself on the beach, of which there are numbers here, and of very large size, there are no signs of animal life. There are no trout to be found in these lakes or in the streams running into them, probably from their muddy and sluggish nature; the whole channel of the river and lakes being a slow, deep, and still stream. In the streams south, running into Lake Ontario, trout are numerous, but the only fly-fishing is in the mill-ponds, which are now, as a general thing, well protected. Formerly, in the Trent, below Rice Lake, salmon used to be abundant, but the sawdust of the mills, and the wanton destruction of the fish, have driven them from their old haunts, probably not to revisit them again, unless artificially hatched and turned into them. Splendid duck-shooting can be had near Scugog village, by getting out on a swamped log or tuft of reeds, sending the canoe away for a couple of hours to beat among the sunken timber, and take the teal or ducks on the wing as they fly past your hiding place. From its easy access and nearness to civilization, this spot affords a more than usual attraction, and only requires to be seen to be appreciated. From the village there is a tri-weekly mail cart to Bowmanville, twenty miles south, a station on the Grand Trunk Railway, and the steamer from Lindsay touches at the little wharf every alternate day, so that if preferable you can proceed thither and take rail for PORT HOPE. This is a very pretty town, lying in a valley on the edge of Lake Ontario, with a very good harbour; the hills rise gradually at the back of it, sloping up to the pine ridges of Orono, and abounding with partridge, hares, and the woodchuck or ground-hog. In the country back of Port Hope, excellent deer-shooting is to be had. The following routes are recommended by a well known sportsman of that district: " Port Hope to Lindsay per rail; Lindsay to Fenelon Falls; portage on to Cameron Lake, and you have the shooting on Cameron and Balsam Lakes, and up the banks of Burnt River." Again, " via Peterboro' to Stoney Lake 17 miles—carry your canoes in wagon,—but the country very wild all through the townships of *Anstruther* and *Chandos*, though there is abundance of deer." In deer-shooting like this, you must have a good tent, with all the necessary cooking things, and at least two Indian or white attendants; three or four good hounds are essential, and of the breed between a foxhound and a harrier; this is considered the best for the purpose, as being generally more compact, and carried in canoes easier and better. Here may be enjoyed to the full by the sportsman the exciting method of *still-hunting*, peculiar to the summer season. When a herd of deer has been discovered feeding upwind, the hunter stations himself in close ambush well downwind, and to leeward of their upward track, and then sends off an attendant in a wide circle well to leeward, till he has got a mile or two ahead of the herd, when very slowly, observing the profoundest silence, he cuts across their direction, and gives them his wind, as it is technically called, dead ahead. This is the crisis of the affair; if he gives the wind too strongly, if he makes the slightest noise, they scatter in an instant, and away. But if he give it slightly, not fancying themselves

Indian Camp on the Road to Lake St. John—(by Kreighoff).

NORMAN, Photo.

pursued, but simply approached, they merely turn away from it, working their way *downwind* to the deadly ambush, of which their keenest scent cannot, under such circumstances, inform them. Of all woodcraft, none is so difficult, none so exciting, and none requires so rare a combination as this, of quickness of sight, wariness of tread, and perfection of judgment. From Port Hope, with the exception of Oshawa, near which there is a large marsh and bayou called "Hall's Marsh," a great resort for ducks, there is nothing of any importance till passing the Scarboro' Highlands and rounding "the Island" with its sandy ridge and belt of scanty trees, we reach Toronto.

FROM TORONTO TO COLLINGWOOD.

TORONTO, the chief city of Upper Canada, lies on the north-west shore of Lake Ontario, facing a very spacious bay, somewhat oval in form, formed by a sand bar or spit, some seven miles in length, stretching out to the west, and terminating in what is called Gibraltar Point, forming a well sheltered and yet accessible harbour. This sand bar has no doubt been caused by the action of the lake water when agitated, meeting the current of the River Don, which enters the bay on the east, and thus, one counteracting the other, they precipitate whatever each holds in solution. Toronto, or as it was styled till 1834, York, was founded by Governor Simcoe in 1793, who, having formed extensive plans for the improvement of the colony, resolved on laying the foundation of a provincial capital, and caused the spot where it now stands to be surveyed. It soon grew into a flourishing town, enjoying every prosperity till the war of 1812. In the subsequent year it was captured by the American army under General Pike, who lost his life at the storming of the fort, which was destroyed by an explosion, causing great loss of life. General Sheaffe, who commanded the British troops, was forced to retire towards Kingston. It was held, however, but a few days, while in the meantime the Government House, the public buildings, and the spoils which could not be carried away were burned. The ground upon which the city is situated is nearly level, sloping gently up from the water's edge to the rear, called Davenport Hill, where from several points good views of the city, lake and bay may be had. This range of hills bears evidences of having been a former margin of the lake, when the waters stood much higher than at present, and the flat site of the city was probably a marsh or shallow. Owing to this flatness of country on the site of the city, Toronto presents at a distance no striking aspect. It is connected by railroad and steamers with all the principal places in Canada and the neighbouring Union. The Grand Trunk Railway, the Great Western, and the Northern, connect it at all seasons of the year with all places of importance, and the country round is fertile and productive in the extreme. The public buildings of the city are numerous, and many of them really very handsome. First and foremost among them is the University, standing amidst the quiet retreats of the University Park, with its splendid avenues leading into two of the main thoroughfares, neatly planted and well attended to. This building, about which many party differences have risen, is Norman in style; its walls are built of white stone from Ohio, and its columns, capital, &c., are composed of stone brought from France. The chief *façades* of the building are to the south and east,—the former of great and massive elevation for distant effect from the lake and bay, with a massive Norman tower in the centre, 120 feet in height. Part of the grounds are appropriated to the purposes of a botanical garden, and close by are the buildings of the magnetical observatory, whose apparatus is very complete. The whole building with its museum will well repay a visit. *Trinity College*, on Queen Street West, standing in a spacious park of twenty acres, is another beautiful building, presenting from the lake and bay a splendid appearance, with its dark background of noble trees. It is of white brick, with stone dressings, designed in the style of pointed English architecture, with bay windows and ornamented gables and turrets. *The Normal School Buildings*, with their beautifully laid out grounds, are one of the most attractive spots in the city, and the building is said to be the largest of the kind in America. *St. James Cathedral*, and the *Roman Catholic Cathedral of St. Michael*, are both handsome buildings, and when their towers or spires are completed will add not a little to the appearance of the city from a distance. *Osgoode Hall*, containing the Courts of Law, is a fine building ; and the *Provincial Lunatic Asylum*, at the western extremity of the city, is well worthy of a visit by the curious in such matters. It is kept in admirable order; and though it is a painful sight at all times to be brought in contact with "humanity so fallen," yet it is pleasing to see the degree of comfort many of the patients seem to enjoy. There is no difficulty in obtaining permission to view it. The Merchants' Exchange also reflects great credit on the skill and plans of the architect. One of the principal thoroughfares, called Yonge Street, extends northwards under that name through a rich and prosperous agricultural district about thirty-six miles ; probably the longest *street* in the world, with the exception of the old Roman roads in England.

Young as Toronto is in years, it has none of the associations which render Quebec almost classic, yet it is as proud of its beautiful bay and aquatic sports as the latter of its ancient walls and citadel. One great drawback its citizens have to contend with, in regard to their public buildings, is the absence of any stone quarries in its neighborhood, thus compelling them to either have resort to brick, or bring at an increased expense stone from a distance. There is a total absence too of any beautiful scenery around the city, the only really pretty drives being out on the lake shore road, over the River Humber, and up to Dundas Street, returning through Mimico Village;—up by the Don and Danforth Plank Road, on the edge of the Don River, passing the cemetery, going through Yorkville, and returning down the Davenport road; or up Yonge Street, past the romantic dell of Hogs Hollow, celebrated in the rebellion of '37 as being the rendezvous of Mackenzie's party at Montgomery's tavern, still existing, near which, in some gravel pits, good fossils of the tertiary formation can be found. Shooting in the neighborhood, except in the spring and fall, when a few ducks, and they very wild, may be had on the bay, is not worth looking after. At the mouth of the Etobicoke River, some ten miles west, there is a large bayou affording good duck shooting, but there is (or till quite recently was) only one boat there, and that not easily obtainable. On the Northern Railway, some thirty miles distant, is a "Pigeon Rookery," at a place called Harrison's crossing. Here in certain seasons the passenger pigeon congregates in thousands to breed, and is the object of pursuit to whoever is master of even a rusty firelock. April is the month in which to go out after them. You may leave Toronto by the morning train, get off at Gilford or Lefroy, enjoy a day among the birds, and return with a well filled bag the same evening. But it is only in certain seasons, about once in four or five years that they are numerous; probably the abundance of beech mast the previous year, their principal food, attracting them, and its absence compelling them to seek other quarters. Of fish, the only kind to be met with here are perch, pike, and a few bass (none exceeding two lbs. in weight) in the pools round the island; eels are abundant, which are taken by night lines; but the sportsman need scarcely unpack his rod while staying here. To make up in some measure for this deficiency in sport, the boating here is excellent, and there is also a very good yacht club in existence.

Very good snipe-shooting is to had in the peat-bogs on the Holland River marsh. You go by rail to Bradford, 38 miles, and within three miles of the station good sport may be had. The marsh is 25 miles long. Above the bridge, on the west branch, birds are always to be found in season. There is plenty of sport all the way up to the forks of the river, five miles distant from Holland Landing, and eight miles from Bradford.

About the pleasantest trip to take from Toronto is to visit ORILLIA, a village prettily situated on Lake Couchiching, a small lake of about 12 miles in length, connected with Lake Simcoe by a narrow channel, called the "Narrows." The scenery on this lake is very romantic. To reach it, you must leave Toronto by the early morning train for Bell-Ewart, on Lake Simcoe, taking the steamer "Emily May," which connects daily with the morning train. The sail on this lake is very pleasant. It is much indented with bays, Cook's inlet at the south, and Kempenfeldt Bay on the north-west, being the largest. On this latter is situated Barrie, sixty-four miles from Toronto, quite a large town. Very fine white fish and maskelongé are taken in this lake, which in winter is completely frozen over, and passable for sleighs. On its shores may be picked up many beautiful cornelians and agates. It is studded with a number of beautiful islands, on one of which, *Snake Island*, is a small Indian settlement. On the opposite side to Barrie is BEAVERTON, a pretty village, at the mouth of the Beaver River, where the steamer also touches. But for scenery in its native beauty, wild yet soothing to the eye,—lake, river, hill, rock, and forest, all combined—Orillia is the spot,—to say nothing of the fishing to be had there. This village was first settled by the Indians, but they were subsequently removed to Rama, on the opposite side of the lake. They support themselves principally by hunting and fishing, and the handiwork of the squaws, consisting of birch-bark ornaments, baskets, &c. The latter are made from the inner rind of the basswood and white ash. They are used greatly by the settlers, being excellent substitutes for wicker-work, though not so durable. A visit to their village is a pleasing change to the traveller. In lake Couchiching there are lots of good trout and black bass, as well as pike and maskinongé; and here you may get night-spearing with good success. This is a romantic and exciting sport; each canoe should contain not more than three persons,—one to paddle the others, who are to do the work of execution; and the flood of light, thrown from the "iron jack" in the bow of the boat, and fed with pine knots, familiarly called "fat pine," or with birch-bark, over the otherwise solemnly dark face of the water, lighting up here and there some scathed trunk on the shore, whose bleached branches give a weird appearance to the scene. The wild shores of a dark lake, with the broad glare of the torch—with one figure noiselessly plying an oar, and the animated attitude of another, relieved against the firelight and peering into the water,—form a contrast of light and shade that Rembrandt might have envied. There is no difficulty in getting either boats or accommodations at Orillia, though the latter for a place of such resort are but passable. In the way of birds, especially the larger birds, there are to be found here a great variety. The Bald-headed Eagle, the Duck Hawk, the Snowy Owl, *et hoc genus omne*, are numerous; among them, too, is that most mysterious and poetical creature the Loon, or Great Northern Diver, whose mournful and wolfish wailing is so closely identified with dark and tranquil waters, and grand old hills, with silence and solitude, whose supposed spirit is feared and venerated by the red men, and whose matted feathers accomplish so much good in keeping warm the hunters of the north. Here also are to be found plenty of deer; these are during the summer months killed when they come into the water at night to cool themselves, or to get away from the flies. You cannot see the deer itself probably, but you will see the light reflected on his eyes, like two balls of fire, as he stands gazing stupefied at the torch, when a well directed shot seldom fails to secure the prize. The deer range through the pine woods at night for the purpose of feeding, remaining hidden in the swamps during the day. They are more tame in summer than in winter, and are fond of feeding upon the young green corn in the clearings.

In the early part of the spring, generally speaking, about April, large quantities of maple sugar are manufactured in this part of Canada; and the whole sugar making season is one of festivity. The sudden transition from winter to spring is essential to its production, as the sap is then passing in large quantities from the roots. An incision is made into the tree some three feet from the ground, and the liquid that oozes out is received in a trough or vessel below. When a frosty night is followed by a sunny day, three or four gallons a day may be obtained from a single maple. The Indians around Lake Couchiching make large quantities of this sugar, and from the very nature of the business, the making of it is carried on in an encampment where the trees are plentiful. The hunting season is at an end, so that the men are there as numerous as the squaws. Huge fires are built in all directions, and over them are suspended every variety of pot, pan and kettle. The men lounge about, the main part of the work being performed by the females, who not only attend to the kettles, but employ all their leisure time in making the beautiful birchen *mocucks* or cases for the preservation and transportation of the sugar when made. The sap is brought from the trees to the kettles by the boys. The length of the sugar season is dependent on the weather; about three weeks generally being as long as the sap will continue to run. We strongly recommend every traveller in these parts to bring away at least one *mocuck* of the sugar, both for his own special eating as well as for those of his friends who may be unable to visit these retreats. The Indians have some on hand more or less throughout the summer, and a few fish-hooks are thought more of than money by these children of the forest. The waters of Lake Couchiching discharge themselves by means of the River Severn, through beautiful scenery, into the Georgian Bay; and if the tourist wishes to extend his trip into the genuine wilderness, he can take the steamer "Fairy," which connects here for the MUSKOKA SETTLEMENT, some forty miles north-east, on a lonely lake of the same name, rich in scenery and sport; but here he must be prepared to rough it with the lumberer or the pioneer of civilization, who may be clearing for himself literally a home in the wilderness;—must be prepared to satisfy his hunger with salt pork, and at night to be well acquainted with the yielding properties of a pine floor. From Orillia to PENETANGUISHENE the road lies through a thoroughly sylvan country, but this place is well worthy of a visit, as being formerly both a military and naval station. There is now a reformatory here for juvenile criminals. The village lies on a small arm of the Georgian Bay. The latter, indeed, might almost be considered a separate lake, and not a part of Huron, extending as it does over one hundred miles in length, and being separated from the main body of its waters by a range of islands running parallel with its northern shore. There are calculated to be upwards of 23,000 islands between Nottawasaga Bay and St. Marie River. The longest of these is called the great MANITOULIN ISLAND, and is viewed by the

Indians with great awe and reverence, as being the abode of the Great Spirit. The extreme point of the promontory separating the lake from the bay is called Cabot's Head. Towards the eastern extremity of the island, where the width is greatest, two arms of the lake run so far into the land as to approach within three miles of each other, thus forming an isthmus, and nearly divide the island into two parts. On this the large Indian reserve, the numbers of its aboriginal occupants are annually getting thinner, and the day is not far distant when the ploughshare of the Anglo-Saxon will utterly have despoiled these once happy hunting grounds. The land, however, is not very good here, being too stony for arable purposes; but as pasture land, it is very productive. The village of Penetanguishene is sheltered by hills of sand and rolled blocks, bearing evidence of the war of waters, when this part of what is now dry land was covered with the inland sea, upon the surface of which only occasional tops of mountains and lines of rocky ridges were to be seen like islands studding the vast expanse, as the Manitoulin and its adjacent islets stud the waters to the north.

LONELY ISLAND, Squaw and Papoose Island, Clapperton, Cockburn, and St. Joseph, are the largest among the islands which lie on the route, none of them remarkable except for the wild scenery of the headlands, and the lofty mountains of the mainland, make an appropriate back-ground. After skirting St. Joseph Island, CAMPEMENT D'OURS is passed, lying contiguous, where are several rocky islets forming an intricate channel called the Narrows. On these islands are found beautiful specimens of copper ore, and some most exquisite kinds of moss. The trees on these islands are all scrubby and dwarfish, owing, doubtless, to the scantiness of the soil. The whole of this group of islands, forming a perfect archipelago, have all probably been at one time part of the mainland; but volcanic agency, some mighty convulsion of nature, which seems to have exerted itself with tremendous effect for hundreds of miles in this region, and the denuding influence of the elements have placed channels between them, that in some places are widening with every wind that blows, and in others are filling up and forming shoals. The Indians are reported to be harmless and indolent, too often neglecting the cultivation of the soil for the more uncertain pursuits of fishing and hunting, although a considerably large clearing is to be seen indifferently cultivated.

In a group of islands lying in the Georgian Bay to the north, called *La Cloche*, a peculiar kind of stone is found, which emits, when struck sharply, a sound like a bell; this has probably given the name to these islands. Similar stones are found in Scotland, and have been so arranged as to produce different notes in good harmony.

At about the southernmost portion of the Georgian Bay, in the wide extent of it called *Nottawasaga Bay*, lies COLLINGWOOD, the terminus of the Northern Railway, 94 miles from Toronto, and a place of great activity during the summer, whence steamers run for Milwaukee, Chicago, Bruce Mines, Sault St. Marie, Fort-William (one of the Hudson Bay Company's stations), and other ports on Lakes Huron and Superior. A steamer, the "Clifton," also runs to Owen Sound. Ten years ago Collingwood lay only on the maps of Surveyors, and what few houses there were lay in a small pine clearing. Now it is a town, where shipbuilding is carried on, large elevators have been erected for the transhipment of grain, and huge quantities of freight to and from the West may be seen piled upon its wharves. Here is a pier 800 feet in length, a break-water, and a light-house. There is nothing in the vicinity to attract attention save a few rocky islets called the Hen and Chickens, and it is not a desirable place to remain in, though good fishing may be had in the waters of the Bay around it. Some idea of the value and extent of the fishing operations promiscuously pursued in Nattawasaga Bay may be formed from the knowledge that the average daily take exceeds 1,000 fish, weighing from 1 to 40 lbs. each, and are carried principally to the Toronto market. Most of the larger trout spawn about the islands upon beds of calcareous rock, over which a shifting drift of sand and gravel passes by the action of the waves, where the water is shallow; and from being exposed to the sun, the temperature of the lake is warmer at these localities than elsewhere.

The steamers leaving Collingwood for Mackinaw and Chicago are of a large class, affording good accommodations to travellers.

FROM COLLINGWOOD TO SARNIA.

From Collingwood the tourist, if desirous of seeing the beauties of Lake Superior, than which, during the heats of summer, there is no more pleasant tour, can take steamer for Ste. Marie; we, therefore, will give a cursory description of the scenery on that Lake, which has several remarkable features connected with it. Its waters are so perfectly transparent that they render the rocks at great depths distinctly visible. The temperature of summer is never gained by these waters, they being even at midsummer exceedingly cold. A fathom or two below the surface, it is but a few degrees above the freezing point in August. In the western portion the water is much colder than in the eastern—the surface flow becoming warmer as it advances to the outlet. A mirage is of frequent occurrence, occasioned by the difference between the temperature of the air and the lake. Great difficulties are experienced from this cause in making astronomical observations. Lanman states that its water is heavier than tnat of Huron, which, in turn, is heavier than Erie, and that a loaded canoe will draw at least two inches more water in Huron than Superior. A healthier region does not exist on the face of the earth, the climate at midsummer is delightful beyond comparison, the air is soft and bracing at the same time, and there is not a single individual who has made this a summer trip, whose breast did not swell with a new emotion as he inhaled the air of this northern wilderness.

On the south side of the lake, between Point Keweenaw and the River St. Mary, are the Pictured Rocks, rising to an elevation of from 150 to 300 feet high, without any beach at their base. To the voyageur coasting along in his frail canoe, they would at all times be an object of dread ; the recoil of the surf, the rock-bound coast, affording for miles no place of refuge. In the appearance they present from their weather-worn aspects, being composed of a soft, friable stone, it requires but little aid from the imagination to discern in them castellated towers, spires and pinnacles, and the various forms of architecture. They have been striped with various colours by mineral drippings, and from this probably has arisen their name. Beautiful caverns meet the eye in every direction, and the water at their base is of a deep green colour, and in many places almost fathomless close in-shore.

The prevailing tints consist of deep brown, yellow, and gray—burnt sienna and French gray predominating. There are also bright blues and greens, though less frequent. They are not scattered indiscriminately over the surface of the rock, but are arranged in vertical and parallel bands extending to the water's edge. All of the tints are fresh, brilliant, and distinct, and harmonize admirably with one another, which, taken in connection with the grandeur of the arched and caverned surfaces on which they are laid, the deep and pure green of the water which heaves and swells at the base, and the rich foliage which waves above, produce an effect truly wonderful. The same general arched and broken line of cliffs borders the coast eastward, culminating in *Le Grand Portail*. This is a vast mass of rock projecting into the lake about 600 feet, and rising to a height of about 200 feet. This has been excavated by the action of the water, forming an arch 100 feet in height and 60 feet broad at the water level. A little further on, in close proximity to Chapel River, is the "Chapel," one of the most grotesque of nature's handiworks. Unlike the other excavations which occur at the water's edge, this has been made in the rock at a height of 30 or 40 feet: it consists of an arched roof of sandstone from 10 to 20 feet in thickness, and rests on four gigantic columns of rocks finely stratified, and which have been worn into curious shapes. At the base of one of them is an arched cavity or niche; if the whole had been adapted expressly for a place of worship, and fashioned by the hand of man, it could hardly have been arranged more appropriately. Being at such an elevation, this excavation must be referred to a period when the waters of the lake stood at a higher level.

Those desirous of visiting this scene should take one of the propellers which navigate the lake, and land at Grand Island, from which he can proceed, if the weather is favourable, to make the tour of the most interesting points in one day in a small-boat and return. The large vessels on the lake do not approach sufficiently near the cliffs to allow the traveller to gain more than a general idea of their outline and position. To be able to appreciate their character, it is indispensible to coast along in close proximity to the cliffs, and pass beneath the Grand Portal, which is only accessible from the Lake, and to land and enter within the precincts of the Chapel. At Grand Island, boats, men, and provisions may be secured without any difficulty. The island itself is wild and romantic; the cliffs of sandstone, irregular and broken into by the waves, form picturesque caverns, pillars, and arches of immense dimensions. There are several romantic bays and inlets, protected from storms—which are frequent in the vicinity,—where the brook trout are to be taken of a large size. The forests on it also afford a delightful retreat, while all nature seems hushed—save by the moaning winds and billowy surges of the surrounding waters. The distance from William's on the island to the Chapel is about fifteen miles.

Near the western extremity of the lake are the TWELVE APOSTLES' ISLANDS, which are evidently only detachments of a peninsula known as La Pointe, rising from 100 to 200 feet above the waters, most of them clothed with a rich foliage of forest trees. The waters around them teem with white fish, trout, and ciscovet, which do not appear to diminish after years of extensive fishing. For trout and ciscovet, which are to be taken with a line in deep water, the best ground of the neighbourhood is off Bark Point or Point "Ecorce," of the French. There is a dreamy summer beauty about these islands when everything else in summer is hot and glaring, which gives one a wish to linger around them.

Near them is another cluster of pict.ed rocks, but only about 100 feet high, composed of a deep sandstone. The arches here are almost numberless, and exceedingly picturesque; while from the caverns, "even in a calm," there issues a sound like thunder, which must be terrific when a storm is raging. The two most prominent peninsulas on the north shore are called Thunder Cape and Cariboo Point. The former is about 1400 feet high, and frowns upon the waste of waters like a crouching lion, which animal it closely resembles in its outline. Cariboo Point is less lofty, but is far-famed on account of the hieroglyphics which have been painted upon its brow, in years gone by, by an Indian race now supposed to be extinct. In the vicinity of these bluffs are found large and beautiful agates. The Canadian shore abounds in rocky islands, but there is only one deserving of particular notice, called Manitou Island. It lies in the northeast part of the lake, and is undoubtedly the greatest natural curiosity in this wilderness. It is about twenty miles from the mainland, and about twelve in circumference. The shores are of sandstone, and for the most part rise abruptly from the water to the height of 400 or 500 feet. But the wonder is, that in the centre of this island lies embosomed one of the most beautiful lakes imaginable. It is about a mile long, and the perpendicular cliffs which look down upon it are not less than 600 or 700 feet high. It has an outlet which is impassable for a canoe, on account of the rocks and trees that have blocked up the narrow chasm; and at the opening of this outlet stands a column of solid rock which is estimated to be 800 feet high. The base is probably 100 feet in diameter, and it gradually tapers off to about twenty feet in thickness, while the summit of this singular needle is surmounted by a solitary pine. The lake is so hidden from the outer world, that the passing breeze scarcely ever ruffles its bosom, and the silence which reigns there, even at noon-day, is intense. The lake seems to be destitute of fish, and the island of animals; but gulls of every variety and in immense numbers hover about. The entire island is composed of rocky material, and probably the scene of great volcanic action; it is everywhere covered with a stunted vegetation. It is called by the Indians Manitou Island, and is held in great awe by them, being the supposed abode of their Great Spirit. The traveller through this region will find but little use for his gun on the lake, as water-fowl are not abundant, for the reason that the rocky bottom of the lake affords no plants to supply them with food; but he may bring with him a quantity of fishing tackle, and his brightest anticipations with regard to angling will be realized. Of the game on the land to be found here, there are plenty of bears and elk, and a few deer; of the smaller animals, almost every northern variety may be found.

The largest island in Lake Superior belongs to the United States, and is called Isle Royal. It is forty miles long, and varies from six to ten in width. The northern side is bold and rocky, but the southern has a number of fine bays and natural harbours, noted for their superior fishing grounds. All along the northern shore at intervals may be seen a line of the smoothest beach, as if for the very purpose of affording protection to the voyaging Indians when exposed to the dangers of sudden storms, to which this lake is very subject. About 100 miles from Sault St. Marie is MICHIPICOTON ISLAND, containing two rich mines—one of copper and the other of silver,—which are being very successfully worked. The formation of this island and the adjacent coast is granite, greenstone, porphyry, and sienite, presenting a beautiful appearance. Near the small harbour of the island the land rises 700 feet perpendicularly from the lake, and in Nipeegon Bay, near by, it attains the height of 1000 feet, frowning perpendicularly on the cold black water at its base.

The Cascade of La Portaille, on the south shore, is a stream which precipitates itself from a height of 70 feet by a single leap into the lake to such a distance that a boat may pass between the fall and the rock perfectly dry. The sandstone of the rock has been worn away by the ceaseless action of the water to such a degree that the superincumbent mass rests upon massive arches, and is intersected in every direction by caverns. No wonder that where nature has been so lavish with her handiwork, every headland on Lake Superior, and every river running into it, should be hallowed in Indian story by some wild legend.

All the hills and mountains surrounding this immense lake abound in valuable minerals, of which copper in every form is the most abundant ; native silver is also found there, but the resources of this section of the country are not yet developed. One fact will strike the traveller at once on nearing the mining districts, viz., that all the men, women, and children, without exception, have been crystallized into finished geologists. The broken-down merchant, selling whisky to the poor miner, strokes his huge whiskers, and descants upon the *black oxyde*, the *native ore*, and the peculiar formation of each hill-side. The great word in vogue among them is "conglomerate," and this term is applied to everything indiscriminately as a verb, adjective, noun or epithet. It matters not how limited their knowledge of English may be, " conglomerate" will leak out in some way or other.

The tributary rivers and streams, though none of them are large, pour into the lake a greater volume of water than what forms its exit at the only outlet—the Falls of St. Mary, or, as it is more particularly known, SAULT STE. MARIE. This, probably, is owing to the immense evaporation going on, and which would be much greater were it not for the dense covering of wood and the long continuance of frost in this region. The surplus waters of the lake enter near its south-eastern extremity, into St. Mary's channel, which, opposite the village of the same name, is about two miles wide, rushing over a ledge of rocks in great fury, and presents for the distance of nearly a mile a perfect sheet of foam. The entire height of the Sault is about 30 feet ; the want of elevation on either side has permitted the formation of a number of islets, divided by channels, which are narrow on the left, but widen on the right hand. After the waters have expressed, in a murmuring roar, their unwillingness to leave the bosom of Superior, they finally hush themselves to sleep, and glide onward, as if in a dream, among the picturesque shores of a lonely country until they mingle with the waters of Lake Huron. The village of Sault Ste. Marie, on the Canada side, is a scattered settlement, where is located a port of the Hudson Bay Company. Indians of the Chippewa tribe reside in the vicinity in considerable numbers, they having the exclusive right to take fish in the waters contiguous to the rapids. They also employ themselves in running the rapids in their frail canoes, when desired by strangers. The town of Sault Ste. Marie, on the American side, opposite to the one above described, is celebrated for the Ship Canal, connecting the navigation of Superior with the lower lakes, which, though only one mile in length, cost one million dollars.

The principal fish of this region are trout and white fish, which are here found in their greatest perfection. Of the trout, the largest species is called the lake trout, varying from 10 to 60 lbs. in weight. Their flesh is similar to the salmon in appearance, but not as delicious. The Indians have a mode of taking them in the winter through the ice, which is very successful. Over the hole they cut, they erect a wigwam, in which they seat themselves for action; and attaching a piece of meat to a cord, which they pull up and down for the purpose of attracting the trout, they pick out the unsuspecting victim with a spear. An Indian has been known to catch 1000 lbs.' weight thus in one day. The trout of this section of the country consist of not only the common lake or salmon-trout, but also, and which is most numerous, the mackinaw trout, or namaycush of the Indians, or longe; it is the trout found in most of our small northern lakes. It is exceedingly voracious, and has been known to attain the weight of 120 lbs. "When the steamer," says Lanman, "runs into the crescent-shaped harbour of Mackinaw, the visitor, when he discovers among the people on the deck some half-dozen wheelbarrows laden with fish four feet long, and weighing fifty and sixty pounds, must not be alarmed at finding those fish to be Mackinaw trout, and not sturgeon, as he might at first have imagined." The very size of these fish is an objection to them, for, as they have to be taken in deep water, and with a large cord, there is far more of manual labour than of sport in the capture of them. There is also a fish of the trout genus, peculiar to these waters, called the *ciscovet*, which is delicious. At the Sault, the common trout, varying from 10 oz. to 40 oz. in weight, abound, and what is remarkable, are in season all through the year—a matter not yet fathomed by naturalists, though probably the constant icy coldness of the waters has much to do with it. The best places in which to fish are at the foot of the rapids, casting anchor from a canoe where the water is about 10 or 15 feet deep, though, owing to its marvellous clearness, seeming not more than three, and where the bed of the river is covered with snow-white rocks. A fly or an artificial minnow is the best bait; with such you need never be disappointed in catching a fine assortment. To pass a few hours in a canoe anchored midway between the American and Canadian shores, now looking with wonder at the wall of foam between you and the mighty lake; now gazing upon the dreamy-looking scenery stretching on either side, and far down the river; and anon peering into the clear water to watch the movements of the trout as they dart from the shady side of one rock to another,—to enjoy all this in a July or August day, away from city life and cares, is a treat that can only be realized, never described. In the village of Ste. Marie accommodations and boats can be had, and a stranger is hailed in this lonely country with a welcome seldom evinced in a more frequented resort. Two or three miles from the village are two streams called Carp River and Dead River, which also afford capital trout-fishing; but the black flies and mosquitoes are intolerable on both of them. The white fish, the *ciscovet*, and the lake trout are an article of export from this region, and there is no doubt that the fisheries here will eventually become quite extensive.

Some 36 miles below Ste. Marie, and opposite the lower end of the island of St. Joseph, is the village of BRUCE MINES, the property of the Montreal Mining Company, and a very thriving place; this island is a frontier station for the British, and Drummond Island, hard by, for the American troops. Some of the ores obtained from the Bruce mines are very beautiful to the eye, resembling fine gold. Some 200 or 300 men are employed, all from European mines. After being taken out of the shafts, which are twelve in number, the ores are taken to the crushing-house, where they are passed between large iron rollers, and sifted till only a fine powder remains; from thence to the "jigger"-works, where they are shaken in water, till much of the earthy matter is washed away, after which it is piled in the yard ready for shipment, having more the appearance of mud than copper. It is mostly shipped to Swansea, in Wales, for smelting. To the south-west, laved by the waters from Superior, and touching the edge of Huron and Michigan, lies the beautiful island of MACKINAW, which has given its name to these straits. All the Detroit and Chicago steamers stop here in passing to and fro, and usually tarry time enough for their passengers to take a cursory glance over the island. The scenery here is romantic in the extreme, and it has four natural curiosities, either one of which would give a reputation to any ordinary island, viz., ARCHED ROCK, which faces the north, rising from the water to the height of nearly 200 feet—a superb piece of wave-formed architecture, appearing, as you look through it, like the gateway to a new world. ROBINSON'S FOLLY, a picturesque bluff, also on the north shore, taking its name from the summer residence of an English tourist, which he would persist in building here, despite the warnings of the Indians, and which was swept with its occupant one night of tempest into the deep below. On the western shore is the CAVE OF SKULLS, where, according to tradition, a party of Sioux were murdered by the Ottawas 100 years ago. This is corroborated by Henry the traveller, who, having to take refuge here after the massacre of Mackinack, found himself next morning "reclining on a bed of human bones." The other curiosity is called THE NEEDLE, or SUGAR LOAF; it is a lighthouse-looking rock, overlooking the entire island, and throwing its shadow upon the ruins of *Fort Holmes*, which are now almost level with the ground, and overgrown with weeds. From this point of elevation, the scenery is extensive and beautiful. Looking westwards is Point St. Ignace, the southernmost portion of the upper peninsula of Michigan. Immediately south of it are the straits, about four miles wide. Turning our gaze to the south-east, we see the picturesque " Round Island," as it were, at our feet. Look to the east, and there lies the mighty Lake Huron. Directly north from our place of observation are the "Islands of St. Martin," while beyond them, in the bay, are two large rivers—the Pine and Carp,—which afford abundance of large-sized brook trout. And, lastly, casting our eyes to the north-west, we see on the mainland the two "Sitting Rabbits,"—two singular-looking hills or rocks, so called by the Indians from their resemblance at a distance to the animals in question. The scene from here by moonlight is peculiarly beautiful; out on the lake in the direction of the moon, a broad road or pathway of light trembling upon its bosom. A few sails of small-boats, trying to catch the evening breeze, pass and repass; the vocal song is raised on the waters, and woman's voice borne on moonlight beams to the listening ear, clearer and stronger as the boats approach near, then, again, dying away in the distance, they seem to merge into the mellow rays of the moon. And while contemplating this scene, perhaps a dark column of smoke, like the Genii in the Arabian Tales, may be seen rising slowly out of the bosom of Lake Huron, announcing the approach of the Genii of modern days—the steamboat.

Mackinaw, during the season of navigation, is one of the busiest little places in the world. But in winter, it is completely isolated and ice-bound. From having been the Indians' congregating place, it will soon be a fashionable resort for summer travellers. Its peculiar location, picturesque scenery, and the tonic character of its climate, are destined to make it one of the most attractive watering places in the Great West. The roads or streets that wind around the harbour or among the grove-like forests of the island are naturally pebbled and macadamized ; the buildings are of every style, from an Indian lodge to a substantial English house. There are several large hotels, with attentive hosts, ever ready to contribute towards the comforts of their visitors. There are billiard-rooms and bowling alleys ; in the stores are to be obtained Indian curiosities ; and the Indians themselves who resort to the island, may be ranked as curiosities to those who have never before seen them. Taking steamer here either for Sarnia or Goderich, on our return, we enjoy a lovely sail down Lake Huron, the Canadian side. of which forms one of the finest portions of America. The tract of land called the Huron District, being the north-western part of Canada West, is extremely fertile, and watered by numberless streams, insomuch that in a tract south-east of Goderich, within a space of 30 miles, eighty-seven rivers and brooks take their rise, or nearly *three to a mile.* Yet the whole southern portion of Lake Huron is deficient in good harbours, the principal ones being Goderich and Saugeen. Long sand bars are found across the mouths of the streams, and this is especially noticeable at Aux Sables, the river running parallel to Lake Huron for eleven miles, the space between being only a sand bar. Geologists tells us the cause of this is, that the prevailing wind, being from the north-west, inclines the stream in the opposite direction at its mouth, so that the waves of the lake being neutralized by the force of the current, the sand or mud contained in both naturally deposits itself in the still water. In the north-east centre of this section of the country is an extensive swamp of about 30 miles in length, lying on the very highest land in the district, which feeds most of the streams that run in either direction. This swamp is wonderfully productive of cranberries, and quite a traffic is carried on in that article, which commands a high price in the markets of the United States. The long peninsula stretching out between Lake Huron and the Georgian Bay, terminating in *Cabot's Head*, is an Indian reserve, where are some promising Indian settlements; but it seems a difficult matter for the children of the forest to settle down at all to cultivate land, or practise the arts of civilization. The whole shore, with the exception of the two or three harbours alluded to, is very bold and precipitous, with scarcely any beach at its base. What little beach there is to be found is very gravelly, and the surf beats upon it as violently as if it were the ocean itself, and not a tributary reservoir. Storms are apt to rise on this lake very suddenly, and from the great depth of its waters, the waves attain a fearful size. Luckily the vessels in such case can run into Goderich or Port Sarnia for shelter.

GODERICH, 140 miles from Toronto, situated at the mouth of the Maitland River, having a good natural harbour, and, being one of the western termini of the Grand Trunk Railway, offers great facilities for the transportation of goods and grain to and from the West and North-Western States *via* Chicago and Milwaukee. It is itself surrounded with a fine wheat-growing country, which, together with the lake fisheries, has materially helped the prosperity of that thriving town. Being situated on a high bank, 150 feet above the level of Lake Huron, refreshed at all times by cooling breezes, Goderich requires only to be known to become a pleasant watering-place. All the streams in the vicinity abound with brook trout, and are easy of access, good carriage-roads extending in every direction; and boats can be had for lake-fishing without any difficulty. The railway here connects with steamers for Chicago, Saginaw, Kincardine, Saugeen, and the fishing islands of the Georgian Bay. About ten miles distant, on the Bayfield River, is CLINTON, a small village with lovely scenery around it, and good trout fishing in abundance; also, excellent shooting, such as partridge, snipe, plover, and quail—the latter are very numerous here, and afford excellent sport. At WINGHAM, some 20 miles distant, deer and bears are numerous, mink, fisher, racoon, &c. Wild-cats are found in the cedar swamps, and beaver and otter are numerous. All along the Bayfield River beaver meadows are numerous, which give it a beautiful appearance, much resembling English river scenery.

Proceeding down the lake, nothing of note occurs except passing the mouth of the River Aux Sables, before alluded to, till we reach SARNIA, a small town, the terminus of the Sarnia branch of the Great Western Railway, as well as a station of the Grand Trunk, which terminates at Point Edward, two miles distant, connecting with the Detroit branch by means of steam-ferry to Port Huron, directly opposite. Sarnia is situated at the head of the River St. Clair, near the confluence of Lake Huron, at the extreme southern part of the lake, which is known as Gratiot's Bay. The St. Clair River here is one mile in width, flowing downward with a current of about six miles an hour. A mile and a half north on the American shore is Fort Gratiot, built in 1814, at the close of the war, fully commanding the entrance to Lake Huron, and is quite a landmark to mariners. In both a military and commercial point of view, this place attracts considerable attention. A ferry-boat plies here across the river, which is only about 1,000 feet wide, and runs with considerable velocity. During the season of navigation, hundreds of vessels of every description pass weekly on their way east and west. These vessels are taken through by steam-tugs, so that every day may be seen from this stand-point a miniature fleet on Lake Huron. Here, also, is a large fishing establishment, where, on an average, 1000 barrels of fish per annum are packed. PORT HURON is at the mouth of the Black River, which, running through a pine country, brings down large quantities of logs annually, employing eight steam saw-mills in this place alone. In the township of Sarnia is a settlement of Chippewa Indians, who reside in small log or bark houses of their own erection, and employ their time, when not engaged in lumbering or rafting, in the more precarious pursuit of game and furs.

LAKE ST. CLAIR.

Lake Huron pours out its surplus waters at this southern extremity, carrying in that direction the great chain of communication by the River ST. CLAIR. This river, which has nothing remarkable about it, except the fertility of the country through which it flows, expands into Lake St. Clair, is about 26 miles long, and nearly the same in breadth. It is a very shallow lake, but through it a ship-channel is cut, and kept clear yearly, by dredging machines, from the quickly accumulating alluvial deposit the river brings down. The river discharges itself into the lake through six mouths, each of them running lazily through long flats of mud, clothed with a thick growth of every kind of aquatic and swamp plant, whose roots, matting together, hold the mass fast, and just make a consistency sufficient for the sportsman to stand on, though the whole quivers and shakes with every step. As may be inferred, the St. Clair flats afford one of, if not the finest duck-shooting ground in the world; there, also, may be found the trumpeter swan, the teal, the mallard, the canvass-back, the wood-duck, curlew, snipe, plover, and the birds of prey that invariably hover round these delicious morsels. But, as the best shooting is to be had when the stormy weather has set in, the hunter must be a true disciple of St. Hubert; must be fortified against malaria, ague, and swamp fever; must be prepared to see no bed and enter no house from the time of entering the flats till, satiated with sport, he reluctantly turns the boat's head towards the settlements; running the boat, always a flat-bottomed one, up at night on a bank of sedge, where the fire is built and the meal prepared, he eats with a zest unknown to the denizen of the town; having supped, he inhales the fragrance of his Indian weed, and prepares for the early dawn somewhat as follows: He dons a thick flannel guernsey, two pairs of socks and *easy* shoes, a warm long-waisted vest, and an oil-cloth fisherman's coat at his side for any emergency. For his arms, he has two single-barrelled duck guns, one loaded with Eley's green wire cartridge, 4 oz. weight of B.B., the other with loose shot, No. 40, capped with military caps. He sees his traps all bestowed in the boat; sees that it is clean and empty, that the sedge or rushes at the bottom of it are dry, and then takes advantage of his last contrivance for comfort. This consists of a bag six feet long by three wide of buffalo robe (fur inside), covered with drabbed oil-cloth on the outside, and provided with a running string at the mouth; getting into this, he ensconces himself up to the armpits, reclines himself calmly on his back; is towed to the appointed ground, and then, covered with sedge or reeds, lies *perdu*, with his anchored stools or decoy-ducks around him, nor moves, even to tremble with cold—for that he feels not,—nor gives any sound or sign of life, except when the wedgy squadrons sweep down, heavy flapping, to their wooden congeners, *haronking* hard by his ambush,—when he springs up erect on his nether man, and pours in with redoubled roar the scattering volleys, which fill the air with fluttering feathers,—falling birds.

To give some idea of the sport to be obtained on these flats, the following extract from the *Toronto Leader*, of November 1860, speaks for itself:—"Captain Strachan and Mr. Kennedy returned last evening from a fortnight's shooting in the St. Clair marshes, where they had excellent sport, bagging, to the two guns, two swans, three snipe, five wild geese, and five hundred and seventy ducks (black, mallard, and gray),—weight, 1,860lbs."

Again, the *Essex Record*, of the same date, says that " Rob Renardson has just returned with two others from a shooting expedition at Baptiste Creek. They have bagged sixteen hundred ducks, two bugle swans (one weighing 35 and the other 40 lbs.), besides a variety of smaller game."

After such statements as the above, further comment is unnecessary. Such sport may be called—sport in earnest.

FROM SARNIA TO TORONTO.

The principal of the islands at the mouth of the St. Clair River are Walpole and St. Anne's; all to the west of the former belong to the United States. The channel separating them from the mainland is called " Ecarté," and that running betwixt them, " Johnson's Channel." Walpole Island, about ten miles long, and from three to four wide, is occupied by parties of Chippewa, Ottawa, and Pottawatomie Indians, the settlement having been formed by a Colonel McKoe, to whom the Indians gave the name of " White Elk." At the south-western extremity of the lake is Peach Island, or Ile la Pêche, the home of the celebrated Indian chief Pontiac, now used as a fishing station. Lake St. Clair receives several rivers, the principal of which are the Thames and the Great Bear River. The former winds for more than 100 miles through the richest and most fertile part of Canada, on whose banks are situated London, Chatham, and several other thriving places. From Lake St. Clair issues the Detroit River, a spacious stream celebrated for its beauty and the fertile country on its banks, but, like its upper waters, extremely shallow. At its head lie the towns of Sandwich and Windsor, opposite to Detroit, the central point of the Michigan Railways, and three miles below is Fighting Island, used mostly for grazing, from the rich growth of natural hay found there. After a course of 26 miles the Detroit opens into the grand expanse of Lake Erie, remarkable for several projecting promontories, chief of which are Pt. Pelee and Long Point. Near the exit of the river, opposite to Amherstburg, where is a famed chalybeate spring, whose waters are said to resemble those of Cheltenham, lies the long, narrow *Bois Blanc Island*, formerly well wooded, but whose timber was cut down during the insurrection of '37-8, that the forts might better command the channel on the American side. On the island are three block-houses, and on the south point is a light-house, commanding a fine view of Lake Erie. The country along the whole length of the Detroit River bears a striking resemblance to Lower Canada. For twenty or thirty miles are to be seen the village form of settlement, the neat church and the habitant. The country is very picturesque, the banks, unlike the St. Clair, high and cultivated, and the eye everywhere rests upon fertile fields, well-stocked gardens and orchards, where the finest grapes, peaches, apples and pears grow in profusion.

The whole of this section of the country was made historically memorable in the war of 1812 and the insurrection of '37. During the former General Hull crossed over from Detroit with 2,500 men, and invited the inhabitants to join his standard. The British force on the frontier was nominal, and could offer little or no resistance; but General Brock, hastening westwards from Toronto, caused him to retreat from Amherstburg across the river, and shut himself up in Detroit, where, on the approach of the assaulting British foe, he showed both the white flag and white feather, surrendering the whole of his force. In the year following, the British General Proctor was defeated here, and the Indians, fighting on his side, sustained the loss of their Chief, Tecumseh, distinguished for his bravery and eloquence. The main object of his life had been to unite his followers in a grand confederacy against the Americans. General Proctor was compelled to retreat to Burlington Heights, where he could only rally 200 men. In 1837-8, a party of insurgents seized Fighting Island, and made ostentatious preparations for remaining there. No sooner, however, did the troops approach them than they hurried away, leaving behind them their arms and stores. Ensconcing themselves afterwards in Pt. Pelee Island, they were then compelled either to fight or surrender. Preferring the former, there was a sharp resistance, but most of the insurgents were slain or taken prisoners. Another invasion from Detroit was made at Sandwich, when the barracks and a steamer were fired, and several persons killed in cold blood, till attacked by Colonel Prince, the invaders were completely routed, and such ringleaders as were taken were executed, thus putting a stop to these frontier invasions.

From Windsor, the terminus of the Great Western Railway, between which place and Detroit three steam-ferries are constantly plying, the traveller can take rail to London, passing Chatham, the head of navigation on the Thames for vessels of any size, and where numerous lake craft have been built, the greatest part of the distance lying along the valley of the Thames River, through a rich agricultural district. Midway between Chatham and Sarnia is the village of OIL SPRINGS, in the Enniskillen district, a large and thriving place, only laid out in 1860, and owing its foundation and progress to the great success that has attended the discovery of petroleum or rock oil in the neighbourhood. There are a large number of refineries in the place, and large quantities of the oil are shipped to England and the United States. The oil seems to be distributed over the whole of this section of the country between Sarnia and the Thames, as wells are being worked in many places throughout the district, and prospecting is still going on. LONDON, which has grown from a wilderness in 1825, situated at the junction of the Port Stanly Railway, is a city of fine appearance, of wide streets, running at right angles to each other, and with excellent buildings. The English Church here is one of the few in this country possessing a peal of bells. London is a sort of diverging centre of railways, it being the junction of a branch of the Great Western to Sarnia from the main line, the northern terminus of the Port Stanly road, and having a branch of the Grand Trunk from St. Mary's, connecting it with that line. It is 107 miles from Windsor, and 76 from Hamilton. PARIS, 30 miles from Hamilton, at the intersection of the Great Western and Grand Trunk Railways, is quite an important place. Gypsum, or plaster of Paris, is found in large quantities in the vicinity, and as the necessity for this manure increases year after year, the trade in it will probably become very large. Situated at the confluence of the Nith with the Grand River, it possesses excellent water-power. There are several petrifying springs on the river banks, and a mineral spring lately brought into notice, analogous to the Caledonia Sulphur Spring, bids fair to attract considerable attention. From Paris we would recommend the sportsman to take a team to Simcoe, 28 miles, and thence by a fresh team (21 miles) to Long Point, on Lake Erie, a noted duck-shooting place in the fall. It is a strip of land nearly twenty miles long, and from one to three miles in width, covered for the most part with a stunted growth of forest trees. It was formerly a peninsula, running out from the land in an easterly direction, nearly half-way across the lake; but the water, having made a wide breach across its western extremity, has converted it into an island. On the east end is an important light-house, to guide the mariner on his passage through the lake. As the direct course for Buffalo and the mouth of the Welland Canal passes this point, a fleet of vessels may daily be seen wending their way to and fro, and from the Point both shores of the lake may be seen on a clear morning. A person going here must procure a good punter, under whose charge he must place himself entirely; great sport is to be had here, equalled only on the St. Clair Flats. Ducks of all kinds and geese are to be met with; occasionally, too, may be seen a wild swan. All around the Point, good snipe-shooting also is to be had. For duck-shooting, from a boat, a No. 10 bear gun is the most deadly; in fact, as a general thing, it is the best size to use always. Immediately west of Long Point are seen for some distance *The Sand Hills*, a long range of mounds barely clad with vegetation, whose sand drifts about with every wind-storm like snow. The Grand River, which discharges its waters into Lake Erie, runs through a country scarcely to be equalled in salubrity and loveliness, the land being rolled and well cleared, and presenting more the appearance of "merrie England" than any other section of the Province. The lands lying at the mouth of the river are low and unhealthy. BRANTFORD, on this river, 82 miles from Goderich, and 78 from Buffalo, on the Grand Trunk Railway, takes its name from Brant, the Indian warrior, the renowned Chief of the Six Nations, who, with his tribe, steadily supported the British Crown during the American war. In "*Gertrude of Wyoming*," he is alluded to in disparaging terms as "the fiend, the monster Brant"; but some years after that production, Campbell (the poet) was obliged to apologize to Brant's son, who happened to visit London, as it appeared, on satisfactory evidence, that his father was not even present at the horrible desolation of Wyoming. Brantford, from its foundries, potteries, and machine-shops, has been called the "Birmingham of Canada." Between Brantford and CALEDONIA lies a tract of land called the

Indian Reserve, granted to the Six Nation Indians in 1784 for ever. A number of other tribes, or rather remnants of tribes, have since joined the settlement, amongst whom are the Cayugas, Onendagas, Delawares, &c., many of whom are still heathens. The sportsman will here have splendid opportunities of obtaining information in the adept cunning of the Indian hunter; and the fishing in the Grand River and its tributaries is fair. Should the traveller possess any degree of curiosity as to the manner and mode of life among the Indians, he has every chance here of gratifying his curiosity. Many of them keep up their old customs with great strictness—such as the war-dance, the funeral dance, the dog-feast, &c. The last is such a peculiar ceremony, and attended with such revolting customs, that it is to be hoped civilization will ere long put a stop to these proceedings. The following description of it is from an eye-witness: "The idea that lies at the bottom of the rite is this, that by eating of a dog's liver the heart is made strong. The first step in the ceremony was for the Indians to seat themselves in a circle around a large pole, and devote a few moments to smoking. Suddenly a whoop was given, and the whole party commenced dancing to the monotonous music of a drum. Then broke upon the ear the howl, and in a moment more the dying groan of a dog, from without the circle of dancers. The carcass was then thrown into their midst by a woman. A chorus of yells resounded through the air, the dog was immediately opened, his liver taken out, suspended to the pole by a string, and the dance resumed. A moment had hardly elapsed, however, before the dancers, one after another, stepped up and took a bite of the yet warm and quivering liver. As soon as this was eaten, the same horrible ceremony was repeated, and so they continued until the carcasses of several dogs were lying at the foot of the pole in the centre of the dancing crowd." Here, too, may be had an opportunity of witnessing the game of *La*

Crosse in all its elegance. The supple and athletic forms of the men are brought by it into bold relief, the only ornament worn being paint over the body, which, with the usual exception, is entirely naked. The balls used are formed of a deerskin bag, stuffed with the hair of that animal, and sewn with its sinews. The clubs are about three feet long, and have at the lower end a sinewy netting, not unlike a tennis-bat. With these they catch and hold the balls, and though not allowed to touch it with the hands, it is sometimes kept from once touching the ground for a whole afternoon.

These Indians, perhaps, retain the customs of their fathers to a greater extent than any other half-civilized communities of them, and as guides with the rod or gun, they are invaluable: they seem, however, to be yearning for the hunting-grounds of the West, and we may probably, before many years are over, hear that they have migrated in a body beyond the Great Lakes.

GALT and GUELPH, north-east of Paris and Brantford, are thriving places, though with no speciality to attract attention. Five miles from Hamilton we come to DUNDAS, at the head of the Desjardins Canal, which runs to Burlington Bay. Dundas is celebrated for its manufactories, and for its beautiful rural scenery. It is the seat of many private residences of the Hamilton merchants.

The City of HAMILTON is situated on Burlington Bay, at the western extremity of Lake Ontario, and from its zeal and eagerness has been named "the ambitious little city." It was laid out and settled in 1813 by a person of the name of Hamilton. It is situated on a plateau of slightly elevated ground, winding around the foot of a hilly range, which extends from Niagara Falls, and which here receives the name of "the mountain." It was of great importance, in a military point of view, before commerce thought of it for a city. General Proctor, who was commanding the army of the West in the war of 1812, made this spot a resting-place after his defeat; and General Vincent, after being driven from the Niagara frontier, and previous to his brilliant victory over the American army at Stony Creek, made his rendezvous at Burlington Heights. General Drummond, again we are told, retired after the attack on Fort Erie to Fort George and Burlington Heights.

The streets of Hamilton are wide and well laid out, and the buildings generally very elegant, being built principally of white stone. An ample supply of this latter near the city has afforded the citizen a means of embellishment not possessed naturally by the sister City of Toronto. Burlington Bay is a very beautiful basin, five miles long and two wide, and navigable in all parts to within a few yards of the shore, making one of the most commodious and safe harbours on Lake Ontario. It abounds in pike, bass, perch, and eels. During the winter a number of spearing-houses are erected upon the Bay, and a large haul of fish is annually made. The method of catching fish by the spear is very exciting; the house is rendered impervious to the light, and a circular hole of about a yard in diameter is cut in the ice; the house being dark, renders the water quite clear, and the fisherman can see to the bottom. A small decoy fish made of wood, and painted in bright brilliant colours, is properly weighted and worked in the water by means of a string; around this the fish disport themselves, and the expert spearsman can select the largest, and by a dexterous throw of his spear pierce it with the prongs. Some of the finest fish are caught by this means, as they fearlessly approach the decoy, and appear unaware of the proximity of danger. It is unlawful to catch any but bass, pike, and a few other kinds of fish by this means, as it is very destructive. The best day for sport is after a storm, with a south-west wind blowing pretty stiffly, as then the fish are on the move. The method of fishing with a spear is not so exciting as the fine old sport of angling. It lacks that glorious uncertainty after the prey is hooked, that nicety of handling, and the pleasing oscillation between hope and fear which charms the disciple of the rod and line. When the spear is in the flesh of the fish the battle is over, and it is only a question of sheer strength to lift it out of the water. The spearing season ends with February, after which the law imposes a fine on any person caught taking fish by this means. Hamilton is the chief city on the Great Western Railroad, of which the head offices are erected here, and the terminus of the Toronto branch of that line. On the approach from Windsor is visible overhanging the Bay, *Dundurn*, the handsome castle or seat of the late Sir Allan McNab, formerly speaker of the House of Assembly.

There are several very pretty drives near the city, amongst which are "to the beach" and "up the mountain." Either of these on a sultry summer day, when scarcely a breath of air is to be felt stirring in the streets, and a fine dust, which is the peculiar property of the soil in this vicinity, pervades every open space, hemmed in by the mountain heights, is exceedingly pleasant and delightful; the fresh pure air on the top of the mountain, and the cool lake breeze obtainable at "the beach," are highly beneficial not only to the invalid, but to whoever is able to enjoy them. "Oaklands," also, is a favourite summer resort, which, together with "the beach," are accessible by steam ferry-boats plying on Burlington Bay. Watertown, six miles distant, and Flamboro' Heights, Wellington Square, seven miles distant, "Burning Springs," Ancaster, &c., are all at a distance just far enough to be pleasant, and the roads, which are excellent, run through a well-farmed country.

Hamilton, being a city of such modern date, has no old associations connected with it as a city; the only historical interest it possesses being centered in Burlington Heights, and the places in the vicinity where skirmishing and battles took place. But despite of this, though not equalling

Chicago in its sudden growth and expanse, no city in Canada has so quickly risen into such a permanent state of prosperity as Hamilton; and from its peculiar situation on the lake, coupled with the splendid railway connection it holds, it at some time bids fair to rival in prosperity the "Queen City of the West"—Toronto. Too much praise cannot be ascribed to its merchants and leading men, who have contributed to place it in its present position.

South-west of Hamilton, some 18 miles, lies GRIMSBY, on Forty-one Mile Creek, the scene of some hard fighting in 1812, and at *Stony Creek*, seven miles from the city, a small body of British regulars and Canadian militia, numbering 700, under command of Sir John Harvey, thoroughly routed in a night attack the American army, consisting of 3000 men, killing and capturing great numbers, and causing them to beat a hasty retreat to Fort George, leaving the communication with part of the Niagara frontier open to the British, and eventually thus saving the Province.

The branch of the Great Western Railway to Toronto runs most of the way near the lake. The whole length of the line is flat and uninteresting, presenting at OAKVILLE and PORT CREDIT glimpses of water scenery, and, when nearing Toronto, running directly along the shore of the Humber Bay, till passing near the Garrison and the old Fort, it enters the new Station of Toronto.

North of Port Credit lies GEORGETOWN, on the Grand Trunk Railway. Half-a-mile east of the station is the railway bridge over the Credit River,—perhaps the finest structure of its kind west of Toronto. The head waters of the Credit River and its tributaries swarm with speckled trout. It is no uncommon thing for an expert to take from 100 to 300 in one day. The best ground is "the forks" of the Credit and Shaw's Lake.

Many sportsmen think it necessary to go out for a fishing excursion with their legs encased in high, cumbrous waterproof boots or leggings. This is a great mistake. They are the worst possible things for slipping on the stones and rocks in brooks and rivers, and encumber the general motions of the body. A good pair of dry worsted socks, taken in the pocket to put on when the day's sport is over, will prevent the chance of a cold, catarrh, or rheumatism. When on a fishing expedition of several days, the sportsman, living constantly in the open air, need not fear any of these maladies. It is the change from a house to camp, or *vice versa*, which is to be dreaded on this account. An Indian will tell you that if he goes into a house and sits by the fire, he is sure to catch cold; so do you generally the first night in camp, but by the next night it is all gone. The best description of cloth of which the sportsman's clothes, whether he be hunting or fishing, in winter or summer, should be made, is the homespun cloth of the country. It is strong, warm, and light; and, when saturated with water, will dry sooner than any other description. Flannel shirts form an indispensable item in a wardrobe for the bush, whether in summer or winter: but scarlet is a bad colour for any part of a fishing costume. One of the best means of keeping off flies and mosquitoes, is by wearing a veil of the finest gauze fastened round the cap, and drawn in round the neck under the chin. It forms a bag round the head, and even the diminutive sand fly cannot penetrate its meshes, if the gauze be fine. Old kid gloves, with the ends of the fingers cut off, will be found useful in protecting the hands.

The shooting throughout the whole of this western section of Canada is much the same in all its localities. In September and October excellent sport may be had with woodcock in the clumps of thick alder bushes standing in the meadows, and in the swampy ravines on the banks of creeks or springy ground. It requires, however, a quick eye and a good shot to kill three out of four woodcock put up in the dense and tall swamps in which they find covert. A drive on a fresh autumnal morning through the gorgeous scenery of the fall, and then a day in covert, watching the motions of the lively "cockers," returning in the evening to your stopping-place with a bag containing eight or ten couples of plump cock, conduce to render a day's sport with this game a delightful change from the monotony of town life. The partridge or pheasant, as it is not unfrequently called, the true name of which is the ruffed grouse, is found in the woods all over the country. It prefers hill-sides covered with groves of birch or hemlock and spruce. It is by no means comparable to the English partridge, and, *en passant*, it eats better boiled or stewed than in any other fashion.

Grouse or partridge shooting commences on the 20th August. Wild pigeon shooting in April, and after July, in certain districts, affords good sport ; in the Niagara district, and in the central part of the Huron district, the passenger pigeon still resorts in such quantities that Audubon's graphic description of the flights of wild pigeons ceases to appear overdrawn. The great advent of them takes place about once in five or seven years, and it is a curious coincidence that in the same seasons the black squirrels are most abundant ; the devastation caused by these countless hosts in the wheat-fields is very great, and the numbers that can be killed in a few hours render it irksome to bring home the spoil. For several weeks in the fall the large open fallow grass-fields are frequented by large flocks of golden plover, which stop here to rest before proceeding further southward. It is amusing near the towns to see the excitement attendant on their arrival. Every man or boy who can muster up a firelock is out on the commons to blaze away at them as they pass, and bang! go a dozen guns pointed at the dense flock; then there is a general scramble for the slain, and those who have loaded with perhaps only a little loose powder claim as many of the birds as they ought to have put shot in their barrels. Snipe are plentiful on all the marshes in September and October; for success with them, you must rely on good dogs and a sure aim, and a plethoric game bag will be your reward. Curlew, teal, widgeon, hares, and in the forests of the extreme south-west, where, free from the growth of underbrush, the mighty maples and walnuts remind us of an English park or woodland, wild turkeys, will be the means of varying your sport. But let the traveller take one piece of solemn advice: adjure wasting powder and shot in the neighbourhood of cities or towns; spring shooting and pot-hunters have for the most part extirpated the game in such localities.

A word or two as to the breed of dogs best adapted to field shooting in Canada:—For snipe, quail, and woodcock, the pointer has been decided to be the best; they possess more brain than setters, and consequently greater memory; the lattaer, in a dog, especially for Canadian use, is everything, when we consider the long interval between our shooting season, say from April to October, and November to April again. Setters, from want of memory, get wild, and require almost breaking again. Many persons assert that the setter has more pluck, and that they can endure more cold; neither of these assertions, however, is correct. The only other kind of dog useful in Canada for shooting purposes is a well-bred retrieving spaniel. It is a remarkable fact that in all pointers or setters imported from Great Britain, however thorough-bred or thoroughly broken they may be, they will for the first two or three years be good for nothing here, shewing no keenness in ranging, and constantly over-running the birds. This is attributable to the dryness of the climate, and until they become *acclimatized*, they are worthless except to breed from; their issue will be fit for work at ten months old.

In botanical productions, and especially ferns, Upper Canada is still more productive than the Lower Province. In addition to most of the flowers enumerated under the head of Quebec, we meet here with the Squill, the Canada or Day Lily, the Turk's Cap Lily (in rich low grounds), the Iris or Blue Flag, the Daphne, the Bindweed or Convolus (equal almost to the garden variety), the Canada Water Leaf, the Gerardia, the Azalea (wrongly called Honeysuckle), the Prickly Pear-Cactus (found on the high ridges in Essex and Lambton), the Meadow Sweet, Jewel-Weed, Cistus, the Nymphœa or Water Lily (in great profusion), and the Sanguinaria or Bloodroot, which, like the English Snowdrop, often thrusts its delicate white blossom through a thin crust of snow on some sheltered bank in spring, as if impatient to meet the embraces of the sun,—each and all of these growing, not some here, some there, but diffused universally, lend a charm to the landscape, and afford treasures to the herbalist comparatively unknown in foreign climes.

NIAGARA FALLS.

From earliest childhood the name of "Niagara Falls" is associated with everything that is sublime and grand in nature ; but to attempt to describe it conveys no more idea of the grand majesty of its beauty, than a painting of it does of the sound produced by the falling of its waters. To the traveller entering from the United States two of the grandest wonders of the world of nature and of art simultaneously burst upon the view—viz., the Falls of Niagara and the Suspension Bridge. The latter being the connecting link between the two countries of Canada and the United States, and the means by which the traveller gains access to the former, must first claim attention ; on the American shore, at the commencement of the bridge, is Elgin, and on the

General View of Niagara, from American side.

NOTMAN, Photo.

Canada side Clifton Village, or the Village of the Falls, as it is sometimes called, though the terminus of the Great Western Railway is called SUSPENSION BRIDGE, or NIAGARA CITY. This village has grown up entirely with the erection of the bridge. Near it is a mill, whose motive power is a wheel below, requiring a shaft 280 feet long to communicate with the mill on the top of the bank; this is quite a curiosity in its way. This International Suspension Bridge was thrown across the Niagara River to connect the Great Western Railway of Canada with the several lines of New York State; it is supported by four cables, each of which is nine and a half inches in diameter, and composed of 8000 wires; the towers are 66 feet high, 15 feet square at the base, and eight feet at the top: the span is 800 feet across. The bridge is indeed a monument to the ingenuity and labour of science. It has two floors—the upper for the railroad track and the lower for pedestrians and carriages, a fee being requisite before passing; and when half-way across the view is most striking. Its tunnel-like form as you look through it is most capacious. Looking up the river directly at the falls, a mile and a half off—to see the water hurrying underneath at a depth of 260 feet, flecked with the long and tortuous lines of foam which have floated down from the cataract, and compressed into a ridge-like rise in the middle, boiling and leaping and foaming in its onward course to the whirlpool—the precipitous banks of the river on either side, with a luxuriant growth of pines growing on the *débris* at their base—and, above all, the passage of the cars over the tourist's head as he gazes, produce sensations of dread and a nervous timidity. So solid is this bridge in its weight, and its staying, that not the slightest motion is communicated to it by the severest gales of wind that blow up through the narrow gorge which it spans. Its equilibrium is less affected in cold weather than in warm, and its elasticity is such that after the passage of a train its equilibrium is at once restored. The cost of this mighty structure was only $500,000.

The River Niagara, signifying, in the Iroquois language, "*Thunder of Waters*," takes its rise in the western extremity of Lake Erie, and, after a course of thirty-three and a half miles, flows into Lake Ontario, which is 334 feet lower than Lake Erie. At Fort Erie, the point where it issues from Lake Erie, it is something more than three-quarters of a mile in width, and the powerful current, running on through a level country, embosoms two islands about half-way in its course to the Falls; these are Grand Isle, belonging to the United States, the original seat of Mr. Noah's famous Jewish colony, containing 11,000 acres, and, about ten miles lower down, Navy Island, opposite to the village of Chippewa,—memorable as being the rendezvous of the so-called *Patriots* in '38 under Van Ranselaer, and from whence, with American artillery, they swept the Canadian shore till dislodged and compelled to evacuate it, Jan. 14th, by the superior weight of British metal. Here the two channels formed by these islands re-unite, and the river becomes about two miles wide. A little lower down, at the mouth of the Welland or Chippeway River, it suddenly contracts to less than a mile, and its current rapidly increases from three to seven or eight miles an hour. The course of the river in this part is nearly due west, and its banks begin to rise, first to ten or twelve feet, and soon to twenty, thirty, and fifty feet above the surface of the water. This rising of the banks is not the effect of a rise in the surrounding country, which, in fact, preserves its level in a continuous plain, but it is owing to the bed of the river descending an inclined plane. Here the waters begin to fall back into curling eddies along the banks, but the current in the centre flows smoothly, till suddenly the powerful stream is thrown with accumulated swiftness among broken rocks; and as you watch it, looking from below, it seems tossed with the first shock into the very sky.

It descends in foam, and from this moment its agony commences. For three miles it tosses and resists, and racked at every step by sharper rocks and increased rapidity, its unwilling and choked waves fly back, to be again precipitated onward with great force against the Canadian side, where they are driven back by the high rocky bank; for at this point the river suddenly turns to a course east of north, and immediately afterwards the water is hurled down a perpendicular height of 160 feet into a terrific gulf, 16 miles above Lake Ontario. Goat Island divides the cataract into two unequal falls, called respectively the American Falls and the Canadian or Horse-shoe Falls. Its exact dimensions can be only conjectural; the American Fall is estimated at 164 feet, the Horse-shoe 150 feet. The latter is supposed to be 1,900 feet across, the former 908. The Canadian cataract rolls over a precipice projecting about fifty feet beyond its base, and the falling waters form a curve, between which and the rock itself persons may proceed thirty or forty yards. The RAPIDS ABOVE THE FALLS are far from being the least interesting feature of the scenery. There is a violence and a power in their foaming career which is seen in no other phenomenon of the same class. Standing on the bridge which connects Goat Island with the mainland, the throwing over of which was a work of noble daring, and looking up towards Lake Erie, the leaping crests of the rapids form the horizon, and it seems like a battle charge of tempestuous waves, animated and infuriated against the sky. No one who has not seen this spectacle can conceive with what force the swift and overwhelming waters are flung upwards. Nearer the plunge of the Fall the rapids become still more agitated, and it is almost impossible for the spectator to rid himself of the idea that they are conscious of the abyss to which they are hurrying, and struggle back in the very extremity of horror. But as they touch the emerald arch, like the calm that follows the conviction of inevitable doom, the agitation ceases, the waters pause, the foam and resistance subside into a transparent stillness, and slowly and solemnly the doomed water drops into the abyss.

The best way to approach Niagara is to go upon the American shore and cross at the ferry. The descent of about 200 feet by the staircase brings the traveller, after climbing over huge boulders, and the *debris* that has fallen from above, directly under the shoulder and edge of the American Fall, and within a few feet of the spot on which the water is dashed and broken into spray—the most imposing scene for a single object that he will ever have witnessed. The long column of sparkling water seems, as he stands near it, to descend to an immeasurable depth, and the bright sea-green curve above has the appearance of being let into the sky. The tremendous power of the Fall, as well as the height, realizes here his utmost expectations. He descends to the water's edge, and embarks in a ferry-boat, which tosses like an egg-shell on the heaving and convulsed water, and in a minute or two he finds himself in the face of the vast line of the Falls, and then he sees with surprise that he had as yet expended his admiration on but a thread of Niagara,—the fractional part of its wondrous volume and grandeur. The current at the ferry sets very strongly down, and it is with difficulty that the boat is propelled across the stream. Arrived near the opposite landing, however, there is a slight counter-current, and the large rocks near the shore serve as a breakwater, behind which the boat runs safely to her moorings.

It is computed that 100,000,000 tons of water are discharged over the precipice every hour; and when we consider that this river is the only outlet for all the waters of Lakes Erie, St. Claire, Huron, Superior, and Michigan, some conception may be formed of the immense volume of water continually precipitating itself over these Falls. Major Warburton thus speaks of it, and his description is most accurate: " The mighty river comes rushing over the brow of a hill, and as you look up to it, it seems as if coming to overwhelm you; then, meeting with the rocks as it pours down the declivity, it boils and frets like the breakers of the ocean. Huge mounds of water, smooth, transparent, and gleaming like an emerald, rise up and bound over some impediment, then break into silver foam, which leaps into the air in the most graceful and fantastic forms."

The first impression formed at sight of the cataract from the Canada side is amazement mingled with disappointment; this is invariably the case, and may be traced, in all probability, to the fact of the spectator's looking down upon the scene, and so being unable to grasp at a single glance the majesty of the view; but by degrees, as the eye becomes more accustomed to the sight, the mind, only wont to look upon ordinary phenomena, feels a new train of thought forced in an instant upon it. There is no time or coolness for distinct impressions; much less for calculations. But it is from the foot of Table Rock, or rather what was Table Rock (for it fell suddenly some years ago), that the mind by degrees recovers from its amazement, and it is in this spot that it shrinks at the littleness and helplessness of man, and the insignificance of his pigmy efforts; the mighty precipice towering up above him, and overhanging, for it overtops its base by many feet—the mass of rock appearing as if every instant it would fall and crush him in its ruins—the thunder of the waters—the spray which drifts around in eddies, painted with rainbows, as the various currents of wind engendered in the chasm waft it hither and thither through the sunshine, like the mist on the mountains, or the finest particle of the snow-drift—and, above all, the seeming solitude of this spot, hidden from the busy world,—all and each of these make an impression on the mind that no pen can describe, and probably there is no other place on the whole globe where such an impression of awe is left upon the mind, unless it be the beetling cliffs of the dark-rolling Saguenay.

The water that comes over the Horse-shoe Fall has a peculiar appearance from the light green or emerald colour it presents ; and from the Horse-shoe Fall not being quite circular, but marked by projections and indentations, which give amazing variety of form to the mighty torrent, it falls in the centre in one dense mass, calm, unbroken, and resistless, and the depth on the edge of the leap is computed to be 25 feet; at the edges and the projections it is broken into drops, which fall like a shower of diamonds sparkling in the sun, and at times so light and foaming, that it is driven up again by the currents of air ascending from the deep below. Descending by a circular staircase, after first paying 50 cents at the Museum House directly opposite, where you obtain a guide and a tarpaulin dress to avoid the wetting influence of the spray, the tourist finds himself on a narrow ledge of rock which leads into a cavern behind the sheet of waters called the "Cave of the Winds." It is in the form of a pointed arch, the span on the left hand being composed of rolling and dark water, that on the right, of dark limestone rock, in which are layers here and there of a shining white *spar*, of which a specimen should always be brought away, if it be but to show that you have been under Niagara ; the cave is from fifty to sixty feet long, but from the obscurity that surrounds it, together with the violent currents of wind caused by the agitation of the air from the falling waters, and the slippery state of the narrow ledge, beneath which is a black yawning gulf too obscure for the eye to penetrate, it is a difficult and dangerous undertaking, especially for the young and those who are at all nervous. The depth of the abyss into which the waters pour has never been, and probably never will be, ascertained ; and the mind is left to conjecture the fathomless cavern which the impetus of the waters must, during the lapse of ages, have worn. On the very day on which Table Rock fell, and only an hour or two previous to the catastrophe, the engineer of the Victoria Bridge, with several of his colleagues, was standing on the spot it covered in its fall. Large masses still frequently detach themselves in the spring from the projecting precipice to the great danger of the traveller, unless attended by a guide, who will have previously discharged a pistol shot or two to loosen and bring down by the vibration of the air, any mass that is detached or dangerous. From the site of Table Rock, a gorgeous view lies outspread on every side. Loud and voluminous as is the sound of this gigantic waterfall which fills the air and ear with its ceaseless roar, there is nothing harsh, discordant, or inharmonious ; the sound is symphonious with the scene, full of majesty and overawing like the distant thunder.

In winter the Falls present a remarkable appearance ; the spray that settles on all the surrounding objects, and especially the trees, becomes immediately turned into a coating of ice, which, in the bright sunshine, recalls some of the "*Arabian Nights*" palaces, or fairy handiwork. The huge massive pillars of ice also, which are formed by the continual drippings on the precipices of the river banks, look like emerald shafts. No traveller who passes by here in the winter should fail to view the Falls at that season.

Of course, in such a resort for visitors as this, there are any number of "hangers-on," eager and on the look-out to ease the unsuspecting traveller of his money at every turn, under pretence of showing this or that ; we would strongly recommend him to take no notice of any such offers, and for the service of guides rely on those furnished at the Museum House or at the Clifton House ; and before engaging a carriage, let him by all means stipulate as to its cost beforehand. The Clifton House on the Canadian, and the Elgin House on the American sides, are both first-class hotels, and private lodgings can be had if preferable ; and as the tourist ought to stay here some days to visit the places of interest in the vicinity, perhaps the latter would be preferable. Good lodgings can be had at Drummondville, only one mile distant, and at a more reasonable rate than at the Falls.

Close by the Clifton House is a substantial dwelling of stone, standing on the highest spot in a beautiful park of 20 acres, commanding a full view of all the neighbouring scenery; this was built and laid out by the late S. Zimmerman, Esq. The grounds are surrounded by a fine hedge of privet, rendered impenetrable by the addition of a strong wire fence. The lawn slopes beautifully towards the Falls, neatly ornamented with forest trees and fountains, and is surrounded by numerous gas-lights, which, when used, present a lively appearance. This was the house at which the Prince of Wales staid when on his visit here.

Goat Island, which divides the American from the Canadian Fall, is a bold craggy spot, 330 yards wide, and covered with vegetation, which has been artificially improved by the laying out of winding roads and cultivation. The island has been rightly named, for its precipitous ledges suggest the idea that goats only could originally find a comfortable footing. From it to a small rock called Iris Island has been thrown another rude bridge, and on that island itself a tower has been built, called the Terrapin Tower, from the summit of which a most magnificent view is obtained, looking directly *into* the gulf of the main Fall. Here, also, is a book for visitors to enter their names in, which affords some interesting records of illustrious names and their accompanying remarks. If this tower is visited at sunrise, when the whole cavity is enlightened by its rays, and the gorgeous bow trembles in the spray, nowhere else in the world can such an imcomparable scene be beheld. Within a few minutes' walk, on the American side, are to be found all the bustle and activity of life; hotels and mills of every description, and a busy town. The mills materially mar the scenery by stopping the view, but their commercial benefit to the neighbourhood makes up perhaps for this fault. Contiguous to Goat Island, are Three Sister Islands or Islets, breaking the current on the American side.

After the American war in 1812, three large British ships, stationed on Lake Erie, were condemned, and permission was obtained to send them over the Falls; the first was torn to shivers by the rapids, and went over in pieces, the second filled with water before she reached the Falls, but the third took the leap gallantly, and retained her form till lost in the cloud of mist below; *one fragment only* of her was afterwards found, a foot in length, smashed as if in a vice, and its edges notched like the teeth of a saw. The steamer Caroline, which conveyed munitions of war to Navy Island during the rebellion of '38, was, after her seizure, set on fire and suffered to drift down the Falls in flames. This must have been a grand spectacle to see in the dead of night, the consuming element lighting up with lurid glare in its descent the abyss which an instant after extinguished it, leaving the darkness more impenetrable than before. No fragments of her were ever found. It is said that the Americans were repeatedly warned, that unless the Caroline was withdrawn from this illegal traffic, she would be seized; but as no notice was taken of the order, the British gallantly boarded and took her, whilst she was moored at Fort Schlosser. In trying to tow her across the river, the current proved too strong, and the only alternative was to set her on fire and cut her adrift, which was done, and the blazing vessel, whirling over rapids and falls, came to its doom.

About three miles below the Falls is a frightfully wild spot called THE WHIRLPOOL. Here the current has formed a circular excavation, the water rushing into the vortex with furious impetuosity, sweeps wildly past the sides of the high and perpendicular banks, carrying round and round with a circular quivering motion trees, dead animals, &c., that come within its reach. The rocks are steep, and no boat dares approach it; and the corpse of a gentleman, drowned while bathing not many years ago, was to be seen for nearly three weeks making fearful and rapid gyrations, suddenly disappearing at some point of motion, and again emerging half its length above the flood, like a maniac battling with his foe. Three and a half miles below the Falls is a curious triangular shaped chasm in the bank of the river, known as "THE DEVIL'S HOLE." Into this falls a stream called "*The Bloody Run.*" Not a very classical name, certainly, neither does tradition afford any clue as to its origin, except in the fact of a body thoroughly rifled having in the early days of Niagara been found there. More probably it has been the scene of some Indian warfare, as the same names, one a tributary of the Mississippi and another of the Arkansas, had their origin from the indiscriminate slaughter of buffaloes that took place there in days of yore. One tradition asserts that it took its name from a detachment of British soldiers having been precipitated over it in their flight from an attack by Indians during the old French war in 1759. Below this the Niagara resumes its soft and gentle beauty, flowing through a channel where the rocks rise from 150 to 200 feet perpendicularly, presenting an appearance as if the river had worn for itself the channel it now uses. Seven miles down, the country rises into abrupt and elevated ridges called QUEENSTON HEIGHTS, and supposed to have been "the place of the Falls" in former ages: it is said that the Falls recede about a foot in a year, and Sir Charles Lyell, the eminent geologist, thinks that *thirty-five thousand years* must have elapsed since the time when Queenston Heights frowned upon the Falls. It is, however, certain, that the attrition of such a force of water must act upon the rock, which is only a limestone, and imagination is left to conjecture the effect to be produced on the bed of Lake Erie, should the course of time run long enough to admit of the Falls receding to that point. The present rapids in the St. Lawrence are thought by Sir Wm. Logan to be the remains of cataracts long since worn away, and the formation of their surrounding country furthers that idea. Queenston demands a visit from the traveller both as being the scene of the gallant defence made there by the British in 1812, and for the view obtainable from this elevation. Here it was that General Brock and his aid-de-camp, Lieut.-Colonel McDonnell, both fell mortally wounded, 11th October, 1812. Brock was killed in the middle of the fight, while leading on his men. His last words were, so history tells us :— "Never mind the death of one man—I have not long to live." A memorial pillar is erected, called BROCK'S MONUMENT,—a column 185 feet high, on the capital of which is a dome nine feet high, reached by 250 spiral steps from the base inside. Beneath, in massive stone sarcophagi, are deposited the remains of both the heroes, who were interred first at Fort George, but removed afterwards to the scene of their exploits as a more fitting resting-place. History tells us that the remains of the gallant commander were, during the funeral service, honoured with a discharge of minute guns from the American as well as the British batteries. On the summit of the dome is a colossal statue of the General. This monument exceeds in height any other monumental column, ancient or modern, with the exception of that on Fish Street Hill, London, in commemoration of the great fire of 1666, which exceeds this one by 12 feet in height. The original monument erected by the Provincial Government was maliciously damaged in 1840 by a vagabond named Lett, who had been compelled to fly to the United States for his share in the rebellion of '37, and who thus sought to insult the people of Canada by this atrocious deed. There is no place in the vicinity of the Falls better adapted for a pic-nic than this spot ; at the foot of the Heights is the little village of Queenston, where the river again becomes navigable, and on the opposite side lies the pretty town of Lewiston, nestling in the hills. During the battle that took place here, the Americans, under Captain Wool, having forced the Heights, were unable to hold them, and before a charge of the British, personally directed by Brock, they gave way and fled in all directions, some concealing themselves in the bushes, others throwing themselves down the precipice, most of them being either killed by the fall, or drowned while attempting to swim the river.

The vicinity of the Falls is rich in the classic ground of battle-fields. Four miles distant is CHIPPAWA, a pretty village at the junction of the river of the same name with the Niagara, whose waters being after rains of a muddy colour, have the peculiarity of flowing side by side with those of the Niagara without mingling, like the Ottawa and St. Lawrence. Here in 1814, after a severe engagement, the British forces under General Riall were met by the American under General Brown, and compelled to retire to Fort George, whence, having received reinforcements, they again advanced, and the two armies met a second time in a place called LUNDY's LANE, near Drummondville, where, after fighting valiantly till midnight with various fortune, the Americans were compelled to retire with heavy loss. It is said that throughout the whole war no battle could compare with this for the obstinacy and courage exhibited on both sides, and though each party boasted a victory, altogether too dearly bought, neither was disposed to renew the conflict. FORT ERIE, nearly opposite Buffalo, is also memorable in history for the assault made on it by the British in the same year, but attended with great disaster, from the accidental explosion of some ammunition, which resulted in a panic and the loss of 900 men. The final consequence of this attack on Fort Erie was even more disastrous in its consequences to the British than had been the attack on Toronto to the Americans when a similar explosion took place. FORT NIAGARA, on the right bank of the Niagara River where it falls into Lake Ontario, at the same period fell by stratagem into the hands of the British; a very interesting and detailed account of all these battle-fields will be found in the Second Series of the "Maple Leaves," by J. M. Lemoine, Esq., of Quebec. Fort Niagara has many interesting associations connected with it, as being the scene of many severe conflicts between the whites and Indians, and subsequently between the English and French: the village adjacent to the fort is called Youngstown, and the fort on the Canadian side "*Massasauga.*" Near here is the quiet town of Niagara, 16 miles from the Falls, noted for its healthy position: and it is quite a resort for the pleasure-seeker, the merchant, and the student, who come over from Toronto on a Saturday, returning on the Monday by steamer. The old historical name of the town was Newark.

Before leaving the Niagara district, the traveller should pay a visit to the pretty and almost fashionable town of St. Catharines, about nine miles from the Suspension Bridge. The country through which the road winds affords a very pleasant drive, or, if preferable, it can be reached by railway, it being a station both on the Great Western and Welland Railroads. It is beautifully situated on a tract of table land above the valley through which the Welland Canal is cut, and is surrounded by a section unsurpassed for fertility and cultivation in the western part of the Province. Here the peach, pear, and plum attain almost as great perfection as in the peach-growing districts of the neighbouring States, and from its productiveness, the Niagara District has been styled "the Garden of Canada." St. Catharines is noted for its mineral springs, which are very efficacious in rheumatic affections, and it is quite a resort in summer for invalids from Northern New York and Canada, many business men sending their families there during August, as from its position they are able, by various means of transit, to run backwards and forwards themselves as business or duty compels. The mineral spring has been brought before the public by the indefatigable exertions of Mr. Stephenson. The waters, which are raised from an Artesian Well of nearly 600 feet through limestone rock into the substratum beneath, have borne the test of many years, and their value is recognized far and wide. The water, for use at a distance, is evaporated by artificial heat, in the usual manner; that part which is composed of common salt first settles, and is removed; the remainder is dipped into vats, until the earthy or useless foreign matter subsides, and the clear liquor is then bottled off for use.

No place on the civilized earth offers such attractions and inducements to visitors as Niagara and its surroundings. The climate is in the highest degree healthful and invigorating. The atmosphere, constantly acted upon by the rushing water and the spray, is kept pure, refreshing, and salutary. There are no stagnant pools or marshes to send abroad their fetid exhalations and noxious miasmas, poisoning the air and producing disease. Wild flowers spring up spontaneously on the sides and in the crevices of the giant rocks, and luxuriant clusters of fir and alders cover the islands and banks of Niagara. There are no mosquitoes to annoy, no reptiles to alarm, and no wild animals to intimidate, yet there is life and vivacity. Varieties of water-fowl sport among the rapids, the sea-gull and the swallow play around the precipice, literally hovering in the mist, and the eagle in majestic flight makes its home among the inaccessible islands and their giant trees.

While curiosity remains and constitutes an attribute of the human character, this resort will be frequented by admiring and delighted visitors as one of the grandest exhibitions in nature.

CONCLUSION.

AND now in conclusion, for the benefit of the tourist and non-resident in Canada, we would say a few words as to its climate. The winter, which is generally considered by travellers as an extension of that season at the poles, though certainly severe, is not so unfavorable as it at first sight appears, and its salubrity is proved by its elastic and exhilarating atmosphere. Instead of alternate rain, snow, sleet and fog, with the broken-up roads of Europe, Canada boasts of clear skies, and a bracing atmosphere, and the "whole of the country is macadamized by nature." Few who have enjoyed the merry winters, the hospitality and pleasant society, the sleigh-rides and parties, the skating rink and the "tobbogin," can easily forget them. If we seek European comparisons we find a parallel to a Canadian winter at St. Petersburg, while the summer resembles that of Paris; but the sky rivals the former in clearness. The advance in the temperature of the months may be well illustrated by changes in the animal world; the song-sparrow sings in March, and the robin, while the snow yet dapples the fields, will make frequent attempts at a song. Wild geese visit the north about the 23rd of April, and in Eastern Canada the harsh, guttural croak of the bullfrog is first heard in response to the music of "merrie England" upon St. George's day. The transition from winter to summer is so sudden, that it has been made a subject of remark by all Europeans who visit the country. With June comes the refulgent summer. The mean temperature of that season ranges from 55° in the northern to 65° in the southern parts of the country, but the thermometer often indicates a temperature more exalted than that of the blood. The mean distribution of rain is 10 inches.

But if the spring be short, Canada boasts of an autumn beautifully mild, and lingering on with its Indian summer and golden sunsets until the month of December. The Indian summer is a period of variable duration and of uncertain occurrence. The French habitan styles it—

> "L'été St. Martin
> De soir au matin."

The highly stimulating properties of the atmosphere here, which, all things being equal, bear a certain relation to vegetation, have not only been observed by meteorologists, but also by travellers, especially arresting the attention of George Combe, the author of "The Constitution of Man." New-comers scarcely feel the changes of the seasons for a year or two after their arrival, and the temperate liver may expect to reach an advanced age, provided no accident befall him.

Touching foreign travel, no quotation is more trite than that of Horace, "Cœlum non animum mutant, qui trans mare currunt." But the celebrated Dr. Arnold said, on returning from his usual summer continental trip, that he had proved the shallowness and falsity of it, as he had found a refreshment in drinking in every instant a sense of the reality of foreign objects, and a mainspring given to his thoughts and feelings which he could hardly have realized from well worn and familiar English scenes. English and American tourists have been too apt to think that they could not go through the nooks and corners of Lower Canada without a knowledge of the French language; and that has to some extent acted as a drawback to the beautiful scenery there met with, for the strangeness of a tongue which we cannot use causes more perplexity and discomfort than persons readily acknowledge. But in the Lower Province English and French culture amalgamate, and the English language predominates; all know it, except a few of the peasantry.

As a whole, this country, with its moderated heats of summer, and its facilities for winter travel to spots otherwise inaccessible, which unfold scenery whose magnificence is combined with the most delightful physical beauty; and the sport it offers to the votaries of Nimrod and the disciples of Isaac Walton, cannot but meet the most sanguine expectations of the traveller, the tourist and the sportsman. To all such, and to whoever bend their steps hitherward, either for residence or a visit, we offer

A HEARTY GREETING.

APPENDIX.

The following is a catalogue of the animals of British North America, compiled from the most authentic sources:—

ZOOLOGICAL.

Scientific Name.	Authorities.	Common Name and Remarks.
Neosorex palustris	Verrill.	Shrew.
Sorex Fosteri	Rich.	" very rare.
" Platyrhinus	Wagner.	Eared Shrew, more common.
" Cooperi	Bach.	Cooper's Shrew.
" Thompsoni	Baird.	Thompson's Shrew, common.
Blarina Talpoides	Gray.	Short-tailed Shrew-mole.
" Angusticeps	Baird.	" " not common.
Scalops Aquaticus	Cuvr.	Common Mole.
Condylura cristata	DeKay.	Star-nosed Mole.
Vespertilio Noveboracensis	"	New York Bat, occasional.
" Pruinosus	"	Hoary " not common.
" Subulatus	"	Little Brown Bat, everywhere.
" Noctivagans	"	Silver-Haired " rare.
Ursus Americanus	Pallas.	Black Bear.
Procyon Lotor	Storr.	Raccoon, Canada West.
Gulo Luscus	Goodman.	Wolverine, Upper Ottawa.
Mephitis Mephitica (Americana)	Baird.	Skunk.
Mustela Pennantii	Erx.	Fisher or Pennant's Martin.
" Martis	Turt.	Pine Marten.
" Pusilla	Bonp.	Small Weasel, rare.
Putorius Cicognanii	"	" Crown Weasel, rare.
" Richardsonii	"	Little Ermine, common.
" Noveboracensis	DeKay	Ermine.
" Vison	Rich.	Mink, becoming scarce.
Lutra Canadensis	Sab.	Otter.
" Destructor	Barnston.	" Northern Lakes.

Scientific Name.	Authorities.	Common Name and Remarks
Vulpes Fulvus.............	Rich.	Red Fox.
" Decussatus and Argentatus.....................	"	Silver and Black Fox.
Canis Occidentalis...........	"	Common Wolf.
Felis Concolor..............	DeKa	Catamount, Panther.
Lynx Canadensis	Raf.	Loup Cervier, *northern woods.*
" Rufus	"	Wild Cat, *common.*
Phoca Vitulina..............	Linn.	Common Seal, *Lower St. Lawrence*
" Grœnlandica..........	Mull.	Harp Seal, *Gaspe.*
Stemmatopus Cristatus......	Gm.	Hooded Seal, *rare—Saguenay.*
Didelphis Virginiana.........	DeKay.	Opossum, *very rare, Canada West*
Castor Canadensis...........	Kuhl.	Beaver.
Fiber Zibethicus.............	Cuvr.	Muskrat.
Pteromys Volucella..........	"	Flying Squirrel, *Canada West.*
Tamias Striatus..............	Baird.	Chipmunk.
Sciurus Carolinensis..........	Gm.	Gray Squirrel.
" Niger...........	Baird.	Black " *certain seasons.*
" Hudsonicus	Pallas.	Red "
Arctomys Monax.............	Gm.	Woodchuck, *Canada West.*
Mus Decumanus.............	Pallas.	Brown Rat.
" Rattus	Linn.	Black " *rare.*
" Musculus...............	"	Common Mouse.
Hesperomys Leucopus.......	Wagner.	White-footed Mouse.
" Myoides........	Baird.	Hamster "
Hypudæus Gapperi..........	"	Red-back " *rare.*
Arvicola Riparia.............	Ord.	Meadow "
Erethizon Dorsalis...........	Cuvr.	Porcupine, *Canada West.*
Lepus Americanus..........	Erx.	White Rabbit or Hare
" Sylvatius	DeKay.	American Rabbit.
Alces Americanus...........	Jardine.	Moose.
Rangifer Caribou.............	Aud. & Bach.	Woodland Caribou.
Cervus Virginianus..........	Bodd.	Deer.

ORNITHOLOGICAL.

Scientific Name.	Authorities.	Common Name and Remarks.
Falco Anatum..............	Bon.	Duck Hawk.
" Columbarius	Linn.	Pigeon Hawk, *not very common.*
" Candicans (?).........	Gm.	Gyr-Falcon, *only in winter—very*
" Sparverius	Linn.	Sparrow Hawk. [*rare.*
Astur Atricapillus........	Bon.	Goshawk, *common.*

Appendix. 191

Scientific Name.	Authorities.	Common Name and Remarks.
Accipiter Cooperii............	Bon.	Cooper's Hawk, *rare—summer*.
" Fuscus.............	"	Sharp-shinned Hawk.
Buteo Borealis	Vieill	Red-tailed Hawk, *summer*
" Pennsylvanicus	Bon.	Broad-winged " "
Buteo Lineatus	Jard.	Red-shouldered Hawk, *rare*.
Archibuteo Sancti-Johannis..	Gray	Black Hawk, *very rare*.
" Lagopus.........	"	Rough-legged Hawk, *not common*.
Circus Hudsonicus............	Vieill	Marsh Hawk.
Aquila Canadensis............	Cass.	Golden Eagle, *rare—Saguenay*.
Halicetus Leucocephalus	Savig.	Bald Eagle, *ab'd't in the West*.
Pandion Carolinensis.........	Bon.	Fish Hawk, *common on coast*.
Bubo Virginianus.............	"	Gt. Horn'd Owl, *not uncommon*.
Scops Asio...................	"	Mottled Owl, *not very common*.
Otus Wilsonianus.............	Baird	Long-eared Owl, "
Brachyotus Cassinii..........	"	Short-eared Owl, "
Syrnium Nebulosum	Gray	Barred Owl, *common*.
" Cinereum	And.	Gt Gray Owl, *very rare—winter*.
Nyctate Richardsonii.........	Baird	Sparrow " *not common*.
" Acadica.............	"	Saw-whet Owl, *common*.
" Nivea...............	"	Snowy Owl, *not common, winter*.
Surnia Ulula.................	Bon.	Hawk Owl, "
Coccygus Americanus.........	"	Yellow-billed Cuckoo, *not com'n*.
" Erythrophthalmus.	"	Black-billed " "
Picus Villosus................	Linn.	Hairy Woodpecker.
" Pubescens............	"	Downy "
Picoides Arcticus.............	Gray	Three-toed " *not very common*.
Sphyrapicus Varius...........	Baird	Yell'w bell'd "
Hylatomus Pileatus	"	Black Woodcock. *rare*,
Picoides Hirsutus.............	Gray	Barred Three-toed Woodpecker.
Melanerpes Erythrocephalus..	Sev.	Red-headed "
Colaptes Auratus.............	"	Golden-winged "
Trochilus Colubris	Linn.	Humming Bird, *from May to*
Chætura Pelasgia.............	Steph.	Chimney Swallow. *[Sept.*
Antrostomus Vociferus.......	Bon.	Whip-poor-Will.
Chordeiles Popetue...........	Baird	Night-Hawk.
Ceryle Alcyon................	Boie	Belted Kingfisher.
Tyrannus Carolinensis........	Baird	King Bird.
Myiarchus Crinitus	Cab.	Great Crested Fly-catcher, *very*
Sayornis Fuscus..............	Baird	Pewee. *[rare*.
Contopus Virens..............	Cab.	Wood Pewee, *not common*
Turdus Pallasii...............		Hermit Thrush.
" Swainsonii	Cab.	Olive-backed Thrush.
" Migratorius...........	Linn.	Robin.

Appendix.

Scientific Name.	Authorities.	Common Name and Remarks.
Sialia Sialis	Baird	Bluebird, *in the West.*
Regulus Calendula..........	Licht	Ruby-crowned Wren, *rare*
" Satrapa............	"	Golden-crested "
Anthus Ludovicianus........	"	Tit-lark.
Mniotilta Varia..............	Vieill	Black and White Creeper.
Geothlypis Trichas..........	Cab.	Maryland Yellow-throat.
Contopus Borealis...........	Baird	Olive-sided Flycatcher, *rare*
Empidonax Minimus........	"	Least Flycatcher.
" Flaviventris.....		Yellow-bellied Flycatcher.
Helminthophaga Ruficapilla..	Baird.	Nashville Warbler, *rare.*
Seiurus Aurocapillus........	Sw.	Golden-crowned Thrush.
" Noveboracensis......	Nutt.	Water Thrush.
Dendroica Virens............	Baird	Black-throated Green Warbler
" Canadensis........	"	" " Blue " *rare.*
" Coronata.........	Gray	Yellow-rumped Warbler.
" Blackburniœ	Baird	Blackburnian "
" Castanea..........	"	Bay-breasted " *rare.*
" Pennsylvanica.....	"	Chestnut-sided '
" Striata............	"	Black-poll "
" Œstiva............	"	Yellow "
" Tigrina	"	Cape May " *very rare.*
" Palmarum	"	Yellow Redpole "
Myiodictes Pusillus..........	Bon.	Wilson's Black-cap, *rare.*
" Canadensis	Aud.	Canada Flycatcher.
Setophaga Ruticilla..........	Sw.	Redstart.
Pyranga Rubra...............	Vieill	Scarlet Tanager, *very uncertain.*
Hirundo Horreorum	Barto	Barn Swallow.
" Lunifrons	Say	Cliff Swallow.
" Bicolor	Vieill	White-bellied Swallow
Cotyle Riparia..............	Boie	Bank "
Progne Purpurea.............	"	Purple Martin.
Dendroica Maculosa	Baird	Magnolia Warbler, *rare.*
Parula Americana..........	"	Blue Yellowback, "
Ampelis Garrulus............	Bon.	Wax Wing "
" Cedrorum	Linn.	Cedar Bird.
Collyrio Borealis	Baird	Shrike, Butcher Bird.
Vireo Olivaceus	Vieill	Red-eyed Flycatcher.
" Solitarius............	"	Solitary " *rare.*
Mimus Carolinensis..........	Gray	Cat-bird.
Troglodytes Hyemalis	Vieill	Winter Wren.
Certhia Americana..........	Bon.	Amer. Brown Creeper.
Sitta Carolinensis............	Gm.	White-bellied Nuthatch.
" Canadensis	Linn.	Red-bellied "

Appendix. 193

Scientific Name.	Authorities.	Common Name and Remarks.
Parus Atricapillus	Lin.	Chickadee.
" Hudsonicus	Fors.	Hudson Bay Titmouse, *rare*.
Eremophila Cornuta	Boie	Shore Lark, *Lower St. Lawrence*.
Pinicola Canadensis	Cab.	Pine Grosbeak.
Carpodacus Purpureus	Gray	Purple Finch.
Chrysomitris Tristis	Bon.	Yellow Bird.
" Pinus	"	Pine Finch.
Currivostra Americana	Wilson	Red Crossbill.
" Leucoptera	"	White-winged Crossbill.
Œgiothus Linaria	Cab.	Red-pole Linnet.
Plectrophanes Nivalis	Mey.	Snow Bird.
" Lapponicus	Selby.	Lapland Longspur, *occasional*.
Passerculus Savana	Bon.	Savannah Sparrow.
Poæcetes Gramineus	Baird	Grass "
Coturniculus Passerinus	Bon.	Yellow-winged Sparrow, *rare*.
Zonotrichia Leucophrys	Sw.	White-crowned " *very rare*.
" Albicollis	Bon.	White-throated "
Vireo Gilvus	"	Warbling Vireo.
Junco Hyemalis	Sclat.	Blue Snow-bird.
Spizella Monticola	Baird	Tree Sparrow.
" Socialis	Bon.	Chipping Sparrow.
Melospiza Melodia	Baird	Long "
" Palustris	"	Swamp "
Passerella Iliaca	Sw.	Fox-colored Sparrow, *rare*.
Guiraca Ludoviciana	"	Rose-breasted Grosbeak, *West*.
" Cærulea	"	Blue " *rare*.
Cyanospiza Cyanea	Baird	Indigo Bird, *West*.
Dolichonyx Oryzivorus	Sw.	Bobolink.
Molothrus Pecoris	"	Cow Bunting.
Agelaius Phœniceus	Vieill	Red Wing Blackbird.
Sturnella Magna	Sw.	Meadow Lark, *West—common*.
Icterus Spurius	Bon.	Orchard Oriole, *West*.
" Baltimore	Daud.	Baltimore "
Scolecophagus Ferrugineus	Sw.	Rusty Blackbird.
Quiscalus Versicolor	Vieill	Crow "
Corvus Carnivorous	Bart.	Raven.
" Americanus	Aud.	Crow.
Cyanura Cristata	Sw.	Blue Jay.
Perisoreus Canadensis	Bon.	Canada "
Ectopistes Migratoria	Sw.	Wild Pigeon.
Zenaidura Carolinensis	Bon.	Carolina Dove, *rare—West*.
Tetrao Canadensis	Linn.	Spruce Partridge.
Bonasa Umbellus	Steph.	Ruffed Grouse.

Appendix.

Scientific Name.	Authorities.	Common Name and Remarks.
Ardea Herodias	Linn.	Great Blue Heron.
Botaurus Lentiginosus	Steph.	Bittern.
Butorides Virescens	Bon.	Green Heron, *rare*.
Nyctiardea Gardeni	Baird	Night Heron, *West*.
Charadrius Virginicus	Borck	Golden Plover.
Œgialitis Vociferus	Cas.	Killdeer "
" Melodus	Cab.	Piping "
" Semipalmatus	"	Ring "
Squatarola Helvetica	Cuv.	Black-bellied Plover, *rare*.
Strepsilas Interpres	Illig.	Turnstone, "
Recurvirostra Americana	Gm.	Avoset, "
Himantopus Nigricollis	Vieill	Black-necked Stilt "
Phalaropus Hyperboreus	Temm	Northern Phalarope.
" Fulicarius	Bon.	Red " *rare*
Philohela Minor	Gray	Woodcock.
Galliwago Wilsonii	Bon.	Wilson's Snipe.
Macroramphus Griseus	Leach	Red-breasted Snipe
Tringa Canutus	Linn.	Ash-coloured Sandpiper.
Arquatella Maritima	Baird	Purple "
Actodromas Maculata	Cass.	Jack Snipe, *West*.
" Minutilla	Coues.	Least Sandpiper.
" Bonapartii	Cass.	Bonaparte's " *rare*.
Calidris Arenaria	Illig.	Sanderling.
Ereunetes Pusilla	Cass.	Semi-palmated Sandpiper.
Symphemia Semipalmata	Hart	Willet, *rare*.
Gambetta Melanoleuca	Bon.	Tell-tale.
" Flavipes	Bon.	Yellow Legs.
Ryacophilus Solitarius	"	Solitary Sandpiper, *rare*.
Tringoides Macularius	Gray	Spotted "
Philomachus Pugnax	"	Ruff, (?) *very rare*.
Actiturus Bartramius	Bon.	Bartram's Sandpiper.
Limosa Hudsonica	Sw.	Hudsonian Godwit.
Numenius Longirostris	Wilson	Long-billed Curlew.
" Hudsonicus	Lath	Hudsonian " *rare*.
" Borealis	"	Esquimaux " "
Porzana Carolina	Vieill	Carolina Rail.
Anser Hyperboreus	Pall.	Snow Goose, *rare*.
Bernicla Canadensis	Boic	Wild Goose.
" Brenta	Steph.	Brant.
Anas Boschas	Linn.	Mallard.
" Obscura	Gm.	Dusky Duck.
Dafila Acuta	Jenyn	Pin-tail.
Nettion Carolinensis	Baird	Green-winged Teal.

Scientific Name.	Authorities.	Common Name and Remarks.
Querquedula Discors	Steph	Blue-winged "
Spatula Clypeata	Boie	Shoveller Duck.
Chaulclasmus Streperus	Gray	Gray Duck.
Mareca Americana	Steph.	Widgeon.
Aix Sponsa	Boie	Wood Duck.
Fulix Americana	Gm.	Coot.
" Marila	Baird	Black-headed Duck, *rare*.
" Affinis	"	Little " "
" Collaris	"	Ring-necked " *rare*.
Bucephala Americana	"	Whistler or Golden Eye.
" Islandica	"	Barrow's " *rare*.
" Albeola	"	Buffle-head.
Histriomicus Torquatus	Bon.	Harlequin Duck.
Harelda Glacialis	Leach	Old Squaw.
Camptolemus Labradorius	Gray	Labrador Duck, *rare*.
Melanetta Velvetina	Baird	White-winged Coot.
Pelionetta Perspicillata	Kaup.	Surf Duck.
Oidemia Americana	Swains.	Scoter "
Somateria Mollissima	Leach	Eider " *Lower St. Lawrence*.
" Spectabilis	"	King Eider Duck, *only occas'nal*
Erismatura Rubida	Bon.	Ruddy " *rare*.
Mergus Americanus	Cass.	Sheldrake.
" Serrator	Linn.	Red-breasted Sheldrake.
Lophodytes Cucullatus	Reich.	Hooded Merganser, *rare*.
Pelecanus Erythrorhyncus	Gm.	Pelican, *accidental*.
Sula Bassana	Briss	Gannet.
Graculus Carbo	Gray	Cormorant.
" Dilophus	"	Double-crested Cormorant.
Thalassidroma Leachii	Temm.	Leach's Petrel.
" Wilsonii	Bon.	Wilson's "
" Pelagica	"	Least "
Puffinus Major	"	Great Shearwater
" Anglorum	Temm.	Mank's "
" Fuliginosus	Strick.	Sooty "
Stercorarius Pomarinus	Temm.	Pomarine Jager
" Parasiticus	"	Arctic "
" Cepphus	Laur.	Buffon's Skua.
Larus Marinus	Linn.	Black-backed Gull, *rare*
" Argentatus	Brunn.	Herring Gull.
" Glaucus	"	Burgomaster, *rare*.
" Delawarensis	Ord	Ring-billed Gull.
Chrœcocephalus Philadelphia.	Laur	Bonaparte's "
Rissa Tridactyla	Bon.	Kittiwake "

Scientific Name.	Authorities.	Common Name and Remarks.
Sterni Wilsonii.............	"	Wilson's Tern.
" Macroura	Naum.	Arctic "
Colymbus Torquatus........	Brunn.	Loon or Northern Diver.
" Septentrionalis....	Linn.	Red-throated Loon, *rare*.
Podiceps Griseigena	Gray	Red-necked Grebe.
" Cristatus..........	Lath	Crested Grebe.
Podilymbus Podiceps........	Laur.	Pied-billed Grebe.
Utamania Torda............	Leach	Razor-billed Auk.
Mormon Arctica............	Illig.	Puffin.
Uria Grylle	Lath	Sea Pigeon.
" Troile	Linn.	Murre, *rare*.
" Ringvia	Brunn.	*rare*.
Mergulus Alle..............	Vieill	Little Auk, *winter only*.

The principal part of the birds are migratory, though some of the migratory ducks have been known to remain through the winter.

DETROIT AND MILWAUKEE RAILROAD.

Tourists and Pleasure Seekers will find this a most agreeable Route during summer.

TRAINS LEAVE DETROIT DAILY
FOR

Pontiac, Holly, Flint, Saginaw, Owosso, Lansing, Grand Rapids, Grand Haven, Muskegou,

and points on the East Shore of Lake Michigan.

Milwaukee, Madison, Racine, Kenosha, Prairie du Chien, LaCrosse, St. Paul,

AND POINTS ON THE MISSISSIPPI RIVER.

Two First Class Side-wheeled Steamers, the

DETROIT - - - - - Capt. McBRIDE,

AND

MILWAUKEE - - - - Capt. TROWELL,

Built expressly for this Line, run between

GRAND HAVEN AND MILWAUKEE,

In connection with Trains on Detroit and Milwaukee Railroad, and at Milwaukee with Trains on Milwaukee and St. Paul, Milwaukee and Prairie du Chien, and Milwaukee and Chicago Railroads.

GOING EAST

Trains make close connections with Great Western and Grand Trunk Railways for all parts of

CANADA AND EASTERN STATES;

also with Line of Steamers for

CLEVELAND, CINCINNATI, &C.

☞ For particulars, see Company's Time Tables, to be had on application at any of the Ticket Offices.

GENERAL OFFICES, Detroit, 1866.

THOMAS BELL, *General Supt.*

THE OIL REGION OF CANADA WEST.

The Oil District of Canada lies in the peninsula dividing Lakes Huron and Erie, in the extreme South-Western part of Canada.

OIL SPRINGS,

a Village of about 2,500 inhabitants, is the centre of the oil bearing districts so far as now ascertained, and is distant from SARNIA, on the Grand Trunk Railway, about 18 miles. The Plank-road between SARNIA and OIL SPRINGS is the best in the Province, and equal to any upon the American Continent. The Stages of Messrs. PETTEE, COOPER & Co. run in direct connection with all Express Trains on the Grand Trunk Railway, four times daily, thus affording Passengers ample facilities for reaching the most attractive and productive portions of the

WONDERFUL OIL REGION.

There are three principal commercial centres in the Oil District, to wit:

OIL SPRINGS, PETROLIA AND BOTHWELL,

but Oil is found at ALVISTON MILLS, |in the Township of BROOKE, in large quantities, and has been discovered as far East as DELAWARE. In fact, the whole peninsula between Lakes Huron and Erie would seem to be impregnated with oil. The Townships of

ENNISKILLEN, BROOKE, DAWN, MOORE, SOMBRA, EUPHEMIA and ZONE

have been, and are being explored and developed by eager, active men, searching for hidden treasures, and thus far their labors have not been in vain. *No Well, so far as we are informed, has, as yet, been sunk within the district which has not yielded oil* This is more than can be said of any other oil bearing region now known. The oil district of CANADA would appear to be the *most productive* in the world.

The oil of CANADA is superior to that of PENNSYLVANIA, on account of its greater density; *the same quantity, when properly refined, lasting twice as long for illuminating purposes.* Again, the value of the oil produced in CANADA may be compared with that of PENNSYLVANIA by reference to the following tables taken from official data, viz:

THE RELATIVE GRAVITY OF THE OILS IS:

PENNSYLVANIA, from	42° to 45°
CANADA	32° to 38°

THE PERCENTAGE OF REFINED REALIZED FROM CRUDE IS:

PENNSYLVANIA	48 per cent.
CANADA	80 "

In CANADA all business is conducted upon a *specie* basis, yet CANADIAN Oil commands at the wells, in GOLD, almost as much as PENNSYLVANIA Oil is worth delivered in the City of New York.

The Grand Trunk Railway Company have an Agent in the Oil region (GARDNER S. CUTTING, Esq.) located at Sarnia, who is an experienced "oil man," and who will give to Passengers any information required, and afford them all facilities in his power for visiting the Oil districts of CANADA WEST.

ROYAL
INSURANCE COMPANY.
FIRE AND LIFE.

CAPITAL - - - TWO MILLIONS STERLING

FIRE DEPARTMENT.

Nearly the Largest Insurance Company in the World.

ANNUAL INCOME £500,000.
Invested Funds in hand to meet Claims, over £800,000

ADVANTAGES TO FIRE INSURERS.

The Company is enabled to direct the attention of the Public to the advantages afforded in this branch.
- 1st. Security unquestionable.
- 2nd. Revenue of almost unexampled magnitude.
- 3rd. Every description of property insured at moderate rates.
- 4th. Promptitude and Liberality of Settlement.

FIRE DEPARTMENT.

LARGE LIFE BONUSES DECLARED IN 1855 AND 1860.

Two per cent. per Annum on Sum Assured.

Being *THE LARGEST BONUS* ever continuously declared by any Office.

BOONS TO LIFE ASSURERS.

The Directors invite attention to a few of the advantages the ROYAL offers to its Life Assurers:—
- 1st. The Guarantee of an ample Capital, and Exemption of the Assured from Liability of Partnership.
- 2nd. Moderate Premiums.
- 3rd. Small charge for management.
- 4th. Prompt Settlement of Claims.
- 5th Days of grace allowed with the most liberal interpretation.
- 6th Large participation of Profits by the Assured, amounting to **TWO-THIRDS** of their net amount, every five years, to Policies then two entire years in existence.

H. L. ROUTH, *Agent*, MONTREAL.

MESSRS. FORSYTH, BELL & CO., *Agents*, QUEBEC.

MR. GEO. B. HOULISTON	- - *Three Rivers*	MR. R. A. YOUNG	- -	*Aylmer*
MR. JAMES MORGAN -	- - *Sorel.*	MR. JOHN DOWSLEY	- - -	*Prescott*
MR. W. COOTE	- - *St. Johns*	MR. GEO. EASTON	- - -	*Brockville*
MR. R. J. LONSDELL	- - *Lennoxville*	MESSRS. DEACON & MORRIS	- -	*Perth*
MR. ANDREW THOMSON	- - *Belleville*	MR. M. W. STRANGE	- -	*Kingston*
MR. HENRY J. FREIL	- - *Ottawa*			

F. H. HEWARD, *Agent*, TORONTO.

MR. W. BELLHOUSE	- *Hamilton*	MR. F. B. BEDDOME - - - -	*London*
	MR. G. M. GOODEVE -	- - - *Cobourg.*	

LIFE AND ACCIDENT.

THE ORIGINAL
Travelers' Insurance Company
OF HARTFORD, CONN.,

INSURES AGAINST

ACCIDENTS

OF EVERY DESCRIPTION,

CAUSING BODILY INJURY OR LOSS OF LIFE.

CASH CAPITAL - - - - $500,000
With a Surplus of over $100,000.

The TRAVELLERS' INSURANCE COMPANY, OF HARTFORD, CONN., was the first to successfully introduce in this country the practice of INSURANCE AGAINST ACCIDENTS, of whatever kind, whether they occur in travelling, or in hunting, fishing, sailing, riding, skating, in the street, store, office, or while working in shops, mills, factories, or on the farm.

A General Accident Policy covers every possible form of casualty, including the risk in travelling, also all forms of dislocations, broken bones, ruptured tendons, sprains, concussions, crushings, bruises, cuts, stabs, gunshot wounds, poisoned wounds, burns and scalds, freezing, bites of dogs, unprovoked assaults by burglars, robbers or murderers, the action of lightning or sun stroke, the effects of explosions, chemicals, floods and earthquakes, suffocation by drowning or choking.

This Company has been in successful operation since April 1, 1864, and up to April 1, 1866, had issued over *forty-five thousand* policies, and paid over *fourteen hundred* losses —in addition to the large sum of $92,500 realized to twenty-nine policy-holders, for $542 received in premiums.

JAS. G. BATTERSON, *President.*
RODNEY DENNIS, *Secretary.*
GEO. W. CAMPBELL, M. D., Montreal, Medical and Surgical Adviser for Canada.
A. B. CHAFFEE, Montreal, General Agent for Canada.

☞ Agencies of the TRAVELLERS OF HARTFORD in all principal towns and cities of the United States and Canadas, where Policies can be obtained without delay.

ST. LAWRENCE HALL,
GREAT ST. JAMES STREET,
MONTREAL.

H. HOGAN, ... PROPRIETOR.

This First Class Hotel, the largest in Montreal, and which has long been regarded by the Travelling Public as the most popular and fashionable resort, is situated opposite the Post Office, and contiguous to the Banks, French Cathedral or Church Ville Marie, the Champ de Mars, where the Troops are reviewed, and other Public Institutions. It has been under the charge of its present Proprietor for over fifteen years. A large part of the Hall was engaged by the Government for the Suite of His Royal Highness the Prince of Wales, on his visit to this city. The Proprietor would take this opportunity of thanking his numerous friends for past favors, and to inform them that he has during the past winter built a large addition to the Hall, and hopes in future to be able to accommodate all who may favor his establishment.

Telegraphic communication from the Hotel.

THE
RUSSELL HOUSE,
OTTAWA.

THIS ESTABLISHMENT IS SITUATED ON THE

CORNER OF SPARKS AND ELGIN STREETS,

IN THE VERY CENTRE OF THE CITY,

and in the immediate neighborhood of the Parliament and Departmental Buildings, the Post Office, the Custom House, the City Hall, the Theatre, the Telegraph Offices, and the different Banks.

It is fitted up and conducted with every regard to comfort; and with certain extensive additions, which will be completed in October, it

WILL ACCOMMODATE NO FEWER THAN 250 GUESTS,

Thus constituting it one of the largest Hotels in Canada.

JAMES A. GOUIN, *Proprietor.*

OPPOSITE THE OTTAWA HOTEL, MONTREAL.

COWAN & CO.'S
WEST END HABERDASHERY ESTABLISHMENT
151 GREAT ST. JAMES STREET.

GENTS' SCARFS, GENTS' KID GLOVES, UNDERCLOTHING, HOSIERY, BRACES
FANCY FLANNEL SHIRTS, &c.

WHITE DRESS SHIRTS ALWAYS ON HAND, OR MADE TO ORDER.

PRINTING HOUSE.

THE Undersigned, having removed into their new and much more extensive and commodious premises, have been enabled to make great additions to their printing machinery and stock of type.

They have now FIVE STEAM PRINTING besides other kinds of PRESSES, which enable them to strike off a very large number of impressions, with the greatest despatch.

Any orders sent by mail, from the country, will be promptly attended to, and forwarded by mail or express.

They have the newest styles of type for handbills and posters.

They will give particular attention to the printing of legal, municipal and assessment forms, guaranteeing at once despatch and correctness.

They have recently purchased one of the COUPON PRESSES of Messrs. SANFORD, HARROUN & Co., the only one of the kind in Canada, by means of which they are enabled to print NUMBERED *Railroad Tickets, Steamboat Tickets, Concert Tickets, &c.*

Remittances from the country in duly registed letters will be at our risk.

M. LONGMOORE & CO.,
Printing House,
31 Great St. James Street,
Montreal.

CANADIAN INLAND STEAM NAVIGATION COMPANY.

ROYAL MAIL THROUGH LINE
FOR
Beauharnois, Cornwall, Prescott, Brockville, Gananoque, Kingston, Cobourg, Port Hope, Darlington, Toronto, and Hamilton.

☞ **Direct Without Transhipment.**

This magnificent Line is composed of the following First Class Steamers, viz:

GRECIAN	[New—Iron]	CAPTAIN	**HAMILTON**
SPARTAN	do.	"	**HOWARD**
PASSPORT	do.	"	**KELLEY**
MAGNET	do.	"	**FAIRGRIEVE**
KINGSTON	do.	"	**DUNLOP**
CHAMPION		"	**SINCLAIR**
BANSHEE	[Rebuilt]		

One of which leaves the CANAL BASIN, Montreal, at 9 o'clock every morning (Sundays excepted) and LACHINE on the arrival of the Train Leaving the Bonaventure Street Station at noon for

HAMILTON AND INTERMEDIATE PORTS,
CONNECTING AT PRESCOTT AND BROCKVILLE
With the Railways for
Ottawa City, Kemptville, Perth, Arnprior, &c.

At TORONTO AND HAMILTON
With the Railways for
Collingwood, Stratford, London, Chatham, Sarnia, Detroit, Chicago, Milwaukee, Galena, Green Bay, St. Paul, &c.

And with the
STEAMER CITY OF TORONTO
For Niagara, Lewiston, Niagara Falls, Buffalo, Cleveland, Toledo, Cincinnati, &c.

The Steamers of this Line are unequalled, and from the completeness of the arrangements, present advantages to Travellers which none other can afford.

They pass through ALL THE RAPIDS OF THE ST. LAWRENCE and the beautiful scenery of the Lake of the THOUSAND ISLANDS by DAYLIGHT.

The greatest dispatch given to Freight, while the Rates are as low as by the ordinary Freight Boats. Through Rates over the Great Western Railway given.

Through Tickets, with any information, may be obtained of D. McLean, at the Hotels, Peter Farrell, at the Freight Office, Canal Basin, and at the Office, No. 73 Great St. James Street.

ALEX. MILLOY,

Montreal, 1st May, 1866.

Agent.

1866 PLEASURE TRAVEL **1866**

LAKE ONTARIO AND RIVER ST. LAWRENCE!

AMERICAN EXPRESS LINE STEAMERS

The splendid Steamers of this Line having been refitted and refurnished, will during the season of pleasure travel, commence daily trips between

NIAGARA FALLS, LEWISTON, TORONTO,
MONTREAL and QUEBEC.

FOR RIVER SAGUENAY, TROY, ALBANY, PORTLAND & NEW YORK

Via Grand Trunk Railway, Lake Champlain, Lake George, White and Franconia Mountains, and Lake Memphremagog,

TOUCHING AT

CHARLOTTE, OSWEGO, KINGSTON, CLAYTON,
ALEXANDRIA BAY,

(Fishing Grounds of St. Lawrence,)

BROCKVILLE & OGDENSBURGH,

PASSING THE

Thousand Islands and Rapids of the St. Lawrence and Victoria Bridge by Daylight.

TIME TABLE.

DOWNWARDS:
Leave Toronto, Daily, Sundays excepted, 6.00 A.M.
" Lewiston, Daily, " " 10.30 A.M.
" Niagara, Daily, " " 10.50 A.M.
" Charlotte, Daily, " " 6.00 P.M.
" Oswego, Daily, " " 11.00 P.M.
" Kingston, Daily, Mondays excepted 4.00 A.M.

TOUCHING AT CLAYTON AND ALEX. BAY.
Fishing Grounds of the St. Lawrence,
Leave Brockville, Daily, Mondays excepted, 8.00 A.M.
Arrive at Ogdensburgh at - - - - 9.00 A.M.
And at Montreal, same day, at - - - 6.00 P.M.

UPWARDS:
Leave Montreal, Daily, Sundays excepted 7.30 A.M.
" Ogdensburgh, Daily, " " 1.00 P.M.
" Prescott, Daily, " " 1.10 P.M.
" Brockville, Daily, " " 2.15 P.M.

TOUCHING AT ALEX. BAY AND CLAYTON.
Fishing Grounds of the St. Lawrence.
Leave Kingston, Daily, Sundays excepted, 10.00 P.M.
" Oswego, Daily, " " 9.30 A.M.
" Charlotte, Daily, " " 6.00 P.M.
Arrive at Toronto at - - - - 5.00 A.M.
" Lewiston at - - - - 9.30 A.M.

Trains leave NIAGARA FALLS and BUFFALO daily, and connect with Steamers, both at Lewiston and Charlotte

Tickets can be purchased of M. B. Sheldon, No. 6 Cataract Block, Niagara Falls, M. Randall, 17 Exchange Street, Buffalo, and Clifton House, Niagara Falls, and Owen Lynch, Montreal.

H. N. THROOP, *Gen. Supt.*, OSWEGO, N. Y.

THE
DAY LINE OF STEAMERS ON THE HUDSON RIVER

NO FREIGHT CARRIED ON THESE BOATS.

THE CHAUNCEY VIBBARD,
Capt. DAVID H. HITCHCOCK,

AND THE

DANIEL DREW,
Capt. J. F. TALLMAN,

Will run on alternate days (Sundays excepted.)

The CHAUNCEY VIBBARD Leaving ALBANY

ON

MONDAYS, WEDNESDAYS, AND FRIDAYS,

AND THE

DANIEL DREW

ON

TUESDAYS, THURSDAYS, AND SATURDAYS,

Making the Principal Landings, viz.,

HUDSON, CATTSKILL, RINEBECK, POUGHKEEPSIE, NEWBURGH, WEST POINT, AND COZZEN'S HOTEL,

Arriving in NEW YORK in about eight hours after leaving Albany.

These Boats wait for the morning Trains of the Rensselaer and Saratoga Railroad, which connect at Whitehall with the Steamers on Lake Champlain, (Passengers by which leave Montreal in the afternoon) and with the Trains from Niagara Falls and the West by the New York Central Railroad.

Passengers by this Line are permitted to stop at Cattskill, West Point, and other landings, and resume their journey at their leisure. This is the only Line which enables passengers to obtain a good view of the scenery on both sides of the Hudson River.

Tickets can be obtained at the Offices of the Grand Trunk Railway Company, and of the Champlain Transportation Company, where Baggage can be checked through and transferred at Albany free of charge. A Baggage delivery messenger is carried on each boat for the purpose of receiving passengers' checks, and on arrival in New York, for conveying the Baggage to the Hotel or residence, &c.

WHARVES:
FOOT OF HAMILTON STREET, ALBANY,
FOOT OF DESBROSSE STREET, (near Canal,) NEW YORK.

ALFRED VanSantvoord, *Manager*, ALFRED WHITE, *Gen. Passenger Agent*
ALBANY, N. Y.

LAKE CHAMPLAIN AND LAKE GEORGE.

THE ELEGANT STEAMERS OF THE

CHAMPLAIN TRANSPORTATION COMP'Y

UNITED STATES - - - -	Capt. Wm. Anderson
CANADA - - - - - - - -	" Wm. H. Flagg
R. W. SHERMAN - - - -	" Henry Mayo

WILL FORM TWO DAILY LINES BETWEEN

ROUSE'S POINT AND WHITEHALL,

Leaving Rouse's Point on the arrival of the Morning and Evening Trains from Montreal, and making close connections at Whitehall with Trains for

SARATOGA, SCHENECTADY, TROY, ALBANY & NEW YORK.

The Morning Boat will make close connections at TICONDEROGA with the beautiful Steamer "Min-ne-ha-ha," passing through LAKE GEORGE.

The splendid Scenery of Lake Champlain and Lake George no Tourist should fail of enjoying.

Tickets can be procured at the Offices of the Grand Trunk Railway, on board Lake Ontario Steamers, and at the Ticket Offices at Niagara Falls.

HIRAM TRACY,

Burlington, Vt., May, 1866. *General Supt.*

ESTABLISHED 1818.

SAVAGE & LYMAN,

CATHEDRAL BLOCK, NOTRE DAME STREET,

MONTREAL,

MANUFACTURERS AND IMPORTERS OF

GOLD AND SILVER WATCHES,

JEWELLERY

In all its varieties and styles,

Electro-Plated Ware, Dressing Cases and Bags,

MILITARY GOODS.

ALSO,

SILVER TEA AND COFFEE SETS, JUGS, PITCHERS, CUPS, TRAYS AND INKSTANDS, CASTORS AND CAKE BASKETS, FORKS, SPOONS, &c., &c., &c.

1866   1866

BEAUHARNOIS LINE.

The Staunch and Fast Sailing Steamer

LOTBINIERE

CAPTAIN FILGATE,

Will run daily (Sundays excepted) between

MONTREAL & BEAUHARNOIS

She will leave BEAUHARNOIS at 7.15 A.M., and returning will leave the CANAL BASIN, MONTREAL, at 1.00 P M.

Charges for Passengers and Freight very Moderate.

LACHINE RAPIDS.

Arrangements have been made by which Excursion Tickets are now issued daily from

MONTREAL TO LACHINE

by Railway, and back by the Steamer Lotbiniere.

The Train leaves Bonaventure Street Depot at 9.00 A.M. and connects at Lachine with the Steamer, which leaves there at 9.30 A.M.,

SHOOTS THE LACHINE RAPIDS

(the finest of the St. Lawrence)

passes under the mammoth Victoria Bridge, and reaches Montreal a little after 10.00 A.M.

THIS IS A DELIGHTFUL TRIP.

Tickets for the Round Journey 50 Cents,

to be obtained at the Grand Trunk Railway Ticket Office, Montreal.

THE OTTAWA RIVER
NAVIGATION COMPANY'S MAIL STEAMERS.

MONTREAL TO OTTAWA CITY DAILY,
[Sundays excepted,]

Stopping at St. Anns, Como, Hudson, Point-aux-Anglais, Rigaud, Carillon, Point Fortune, Grenville, L'Orignal, Major's, Brown's, O'Brien's, Thurso, Buckingham.

The Splendid New Fast Sailing Steamers

PRINCE OF WALES, **QUEEN VICTORIA,**
Capt. H. W. SHEPHERD,   Capt. A. BOWIE,

A Train leaves the Bonaventure Street Depot every morning [Sundays excepted] at SEVEN o'clock, to connect at Lachine with the Steamer "PRINCE OF WALES," [Breakfast] for Carillon, passing through Lake St. Louis, St. Ann's Rapids, and Lake of Two Mountains. From Carillon, by Railroad, to Grenville, join the Steamer "QUEEN VICTORIA," [Dinner] for Ottawa City.

Downward the Steamer "QUEEN VICTORIA" leaves Ottawa City at 6.30 A.M., passengers arriving at Montreal at 4.30 P.M.

The comfort and economy of this Line are unsurpassed, while the Route passes through one of the most picturesque districts in Canada, and is the most fashionable for tourists.

Parties desirous of a pleasant trip can obtain Return Tickets from Montreal to Carillon, valid for one day, at single fares.

Passengers for the celebrated Caledonian Springs will be landed at L'Orignal.

PARCEL EXPRESS daily from the Office to Ottawa and intermediate landings.

Further information, as well as Return Tickets, may be obtained at the Office, Mercantile Library, Bonaventure Street, (opposite the Bonaventure Building,) at the Bonaventure Depot, or on board the Steamers. Excursion Tickets may be obtained at the Office, or on board the Steamers.

R. W. SHEPHERD,
President.

1866   TO TOURISTS AND TRAVELLERS.   1866

NEW AND IMPORTANT ARRANGEMENT.

GRAND TRUNK RAILWAY

   AND

ROYAL MAIL LINE
OF THROUGH STEAMERS.

NIAGARA FALLS TO MONTREAL

QUEBEC, WHITE MOUNTAINS,

PORTLAND, BOSTON, LAKE GEORGE, SARATOGA,

NEW YORK, THE RIVER SAGUENAY,

&c.,   &c.,   &c.

NO TRANSHIPMENT AT OGDENSBURGH.

The Only Line by which Passengers can retain their State Rooms through the entire Trip, and passing the Scenery of

The Thousand Islands and Rapids of the St. Lawrence by Daylight.

☞ This Route possesses peculiar advantages over any other, as by it parties *have their choice of conveyance between Niagara Falls and Quebec* over the whole or any portion of it, without being obliged to decide when purchasing their Tickets, consequently should the weather prove unfavorable *Passengers may avoid Lake Ontario* by taking the Grand Trunk Road to Kingston, and from thence by one of the above Steamers, making close connections. No extra charge for MEALS and STATE ROOMS.

The only Route to the White Mountains by which parties can ascend the far-famed Mount Washington by the Carriage Road.

AMERICAN MONEY TAKEN AT PAR FOR TICKETS

by this Line, which can be obtained at most of the principal Cities in the United States

Arrangements have also been made with the Proprietors of the Principal Hotels at Toronto, Montreal and Quebec, to take American Money at Par, charging New York Hotel Rates.

ALEX. MILLOY, *Gen. Agent,*	**E. B. BARBER,**	**C. J. BRYDGES,**
R. M. L. STEAMERS	*Joint Agent,*	*Managing Director,*
Office, Gt. St. James Street,	G.T.R. & R.M.L. Steamers,	GRAND TRUNK RAILWAY,
MONTREAL.	Niagara Falls, N.Y.	Montreal.

GRAND TRUNK LINE.

 **1866**

EXPRESS RAIL AND STEAMBOAT ROUTE

VIA SARNIA

BY THE

GRAND TRUNK RAILWAY

and the following Large, Commodious and Fast Sailing Steamers for

CHICAGO, MILWAUKEE, SHEBOYGAN

and other Lake Michigan Ports, and for all places in the West and North-West.

The Steamboat Line during the season of 1866 will consist of the undermentioned low-pressure, elegantly fitted Passenger Steamers, one of which will leave SARNIA every

TUESDAY, THURSDAY AND SATURDAY,

on arrival of the Grand Trunk Train from the East, and connect at Milwaukee and Chicago with all Lines for the West, South and North-West.

The Boats will run from Sarnia according to the following Table:

ANTELOPE, Capt. ROBERT NICHOLSON, Leaves SARNIA		MONTGOMERY, Capt. A. GILLIES, Leaves SARNIA	
May 5, 15 and 24.	June 2, 12, 21 and 30	May 8, 17 and 26.	June 5, 14 and 23
July 10, 19 and 28.	August 7, 16 and 25	July 3, 12 and 21.	August 9, 18 and 28
Sept. 4, 13 and 22.	Oct. 2, 11, 20 and 30	Sept. 6, 15 and 25.	October 4, 13 and 23
SUN, Capt. R. A. JONES, Leaves SARNIA		**B. F. WADE**, Capt. JAMES F. SNOW, Leaves SARNIA	
May 10, 19 and 29.	June 7, 16 and 26	May 2, 12, 22 and 31.	June 9, 19 and 28
July 5, 14 and 24.	Aug't 2, 11, 21 and 30	July 7, 17 and 26.	Aug. 4, 14 and 23
Sept. 8, 18 and 27.	October 6, 16 and 25	Sept. 1, 11, 20 and 29.	Oct. 9, 18 and 27

Passengers can rely upon the Boats leaving as advertised.

All First Class Tickets include Meals and State Rooms.

Passengers desiring to travel all rail can obtain Tickets *via* the Grand Trunk Railway as cheap as by any other Route.

Close connection made at Detroit with all Lines.

At Refreshment Rooms American Money taken at par from Passengers holding Through Tickets.

SUPERB SLEEPING CARS ON ALL NIGHT TRAINS.

For Fares, Rates for Freight, and all other particulars, apply to the Agents of the Grand Trunk Railway Company.

C. J. BRYDGES,

Montreal, May 1, 1866. *Managing Director.*

RICHELIEU COMPANY'S
Daily Royal Mail  Line of Steamers

RUNNING BETWEEN
MONTREAL & QUEBEC.

The Iron Steamer
QUEBEC . , ... Capt. J. B. Labelle

And Iron Steamer
MONTREAL . . . . Capt. Robert Nelson

LEAVE RICHELIEU PIER, OPPOSITE JACQUES CARTIER SQUARE, MONTREAL,
alternately every Evening at seven o'clock during the season, for

QUEBEC,
CALLING AT INTERMEDIATE PORTS.

FARES:

FIRST CLASS (Meals and open Berth included) - - - - - - $2.50
SECOND CLASS - - - - - - - - - - - - - - - - - - - $1.00

And the side lines of Steamers running between
MONTREAL, THREE RIVERS, AND THE INTERMEDIATE PORTS,

leaving MONTREAL every TUESDAY and FRIDAY:

Steamer COLUMBIA, Capt. Joseph Duval, between MONTREAL and THREE RIVERS, calling at Sorel, Maskinonge, Riviere du Loup, and Yamachiche.

Steamer NAPOLEON, Capt. Charles Daveluy, between MONTREAL and SOREL, calling at St. Sulpice, Lavaltrie, Lanoraie, and Berthier.

Steamer CHAMBLY, Capt. Frs. Lamoureux, between MONTREAL and CHAMBLY, calling at Vercheres, Contrecœur, Sorel, St. Ours, St. Denis, St. Charles, St. Mathias, Belœil, and St. Hilaire.

Steamer TERREBONNE, Capt. L. H. Roy, between MONTREAL and TERREBONNE, calling at Boucherville, Varennes, and Lachenaie.

Steamer L'ETOILE, Capt. P. E. Maliiot, between MONTREAL and L'ASSOMPTION, calling at Bout de l'Isle and St. Paul.

For further information apply at the Office,

203 COMMISSIONERS STREET,

J. B. LAMERE, *General Manager.*

MICHIGAN SOUTHERN RAILROAD.

THREE DIRECT LINES.

DETROIT TO CHICAGO.
DETROIT TO TOLEDO,
AND
TOLEDO TO CHICAGO.

All of which connect with the Trains of the other Roads at above named places, forming the most COMFORTABLE and RELIABLE links in the great routes between the

EAST AND WEST,
SOUTH AND NORTH-WEST.

DISTANCE, FARE AND TIME SAME AS COMPETING LINES,

and all the modern appliances for the

CONVENIENCE, COMFORT AND SAFETY

of Passengers, in use on all Trains.

ELEGANT SALOON COACHES,
LUXURIOUS SLEEPING CARS AND SMOKING CARS,

with improved ventilators and dusters.

THROUGH TICKETS AND CHECKS FOR BAGGAGE

can be obtained at the principal Railroad and Steamboat Offices in the United States and Canadas.

CHAS. F. HATCH, *Gen. Supt.*   GEO. ENEARL,
C. P. LELAND, *Gen. Ticket Agent.*   *Passenger Agt. for Canadas.*

THE OTTAWA & PRESCOTT RAILWAY.

THE ONLY RAILWAY ROUTE TO THE

CITY OF OTTAWA

the Capital and Seat of Government of Canada.

Distant from the St. Lawrence, at Prescott, opposite Ogdensburg, 54 miles.

THE PARLIAMENTARY BUILDINGS,

just completed, both from their position and grandeur of the surrounding scenery, as well as from the beauty of the architectural design, are well worthy the attention of

THE TOURIST.

The scenery and natural curiosities of the Upper Ottawa, the beautiful Falls of the Chaudière and of the Rideau River, the Timber Slides, the extensive Water-power, and the Lumbering and other Mills, which are within easy reach of the City, form a combination of attraction not easily equalled and certainly not surpassed in Canada.

TRAINS ON THE

OTTAWA & PRESCOTT RAILWAY,

which run in conjunction with the Grand Trunk Railway and with the Railways of the United States at Ogdensburgh,

LEAVE PRESCOTT AND OTTAWA

Respectively TWICE DAILY.

FOR PARTICULARS SEE PUBLISHED TIME TABLES.

GREAT CENTRAL ROUTE.

GREAT WESTERN RAILWAY OF CANADA

AND UNITED STATES MAIL ROUTE FROM

DETROIT, MICH., TO SUSPENSION BRIDGE, NIAGARA FALLS,

AND BRANCH ROADS FROM

Hamilton to Toronto; from Harrisburg to Guelph; and from Komoka to Sarnia,

forming with its connections the shortest and best route between all points

EAST AND WEST.

Three THROUGH EXPRESS TRAINS each way DAILY, connecting at Detroit with the Michigan Central, Michigan Southern, and Detroit and Milwaukee Railroads, for all points West, North-West and South-West; at Suspension Bridge with the New York Central Railroad, for all points East, South-East and North-east; at Hamilton with the Royal Mail Line of Steamers; and at Toronto with the Grand Trunk Railway and the Royal Mail and American Express Lines of Steamers for all points on Lake Ontario and the River St. Lawrence.

The only Route via Niagara Falls, and passing directly through the Oil Regions of Canada.

FARES AS LOW AS BY OTHER LINES.

Sleeping Cars on Night Trains, and Smoking Cars on Day Trains.

BAGGAGE CHECKED THROUGH TO ALL IMPORTANT POINTS.

American Currency taken at par for Through Fares and Sleeping Car Berths; also for Meals, &c., at Refreshment Saloons.

Trains run by Hamilton time, which is 12 minutes faster than Detroit time; 25 minutes slower than New York Central Railroad time, and 30 minutes faster than Montreal time.

Through Tickets by this Route are for sale at all the principal Ticket Offices in the United States and Canadas.

THOMAS SWINYARD, *General Manager*, HAMILTON, C. W.
JAMES CHARLTON, *General Agent*, HAMILTON. C. W.

MONTREAL OCEAN STEAMSHIP COMP'Y.

LIVERPOOL, LONDONDERRY, BELFAST AND GLASGOW.

Every SATURDAY from QUEBEC during Summer, and PORTLAND during Winter, at Lowest Fares.

The following Full-powered Clyde Built Steamships compose the fleet of the Montreal Ocean Steamship Co. These Steamships are not surpassed by any afloat; they are commanded by gentlemen of known ability and experience, whose character is sufficient gurantee for the best treatment and utmost attention—the average passages have been ten days:

MORAVIAN,	-	2650 Tons.	PERUVIAN, -	-	2600 Tons.
HIBERNIAN,	-	2320 "	BELGIAN, -	-	2600 "
NORTH AMERICAN	1800 "		AUSTRIAN,	-	2700 "
NOVA SCOTIAN,	-	2200 "	ACADIAN,	-	2700 "
	DAMASCUS	-	-	-	1600 Tons.

GLASGOW DIRECT.

One of the following Clyde Built Steamships leaves QUEBEC during Summer, and PORTLAND during Winter, about once every two weeks:

ST. DAVID	- - - -	1600 Tons.	ST. ANDREW - - -	1468 Tons.
ST. GEORGE	- - -	1468 "	ST. PATRICK - - -	1468 "

THROUGH PASSAGE CERTIFICATES are now granted to parties wishing to bring out their friends from England, Ireland or Scotland to any part of Canada at very low rates. The Steamships of the Canadian Line leave Liverpool every Thursday, and Londonderry every Friday, also leave Glasgow once every two weeks—they come direct to the Grand Trunk Wharf, thereby saving much inconvenience, annoyance and expense to passengers. The Baggage is checked through to destination, and Special Trains are despatched on arrival of Steamers. The rates of passage are very low, the sea voyage does not average over ten days, and the facilities and accommodation given by the Canadian Line cannot be surpassed by any other line of Steamers afloat.

For Through Tickets, Pre-Paid Passage Certificates, and every information, apply to

H. BOURLIER, Agent, Grand Trunk Railway, Union Station, Toronto.

INTERNATIONAL STEAMSHIP COMPANY.

T. C. HERSEY, President. H. J. LIBBY, Treasurer.

Office, 159½ Commercial Street, Portland, Me.  J. B COYLE, G. A., and Chief Engineer.

LINE OF STEAMERS TO THE EASTERN COAST OF MAINE AND LOWER BRITISH PROVINCES

by the First Class Sea-going Side-wheeled Steamers

NEW BRUNSWICK - - - - -	Capt. WINCHESTER
NEW ENGLAND - - - - -	" FIELD
NEW YORK - - - - - -	" CHISHOLM

One of these Steamers leaves BOSTON every MONDAY and THURSDAY Morning at 8 o'clock, and PORTLAND the same days at 5 o'clock P.M., for EASTPORT and ST. JOHN.

At EASTPORT the Steamers connect for Calais, St. Stephens, St. Andrews, Woodstock, and Houlton Stations.

At ST. JOHN, for Fredericton, N.B., Halifax, Digby, Windsor, N.S., Shediac, N.B., Charlottetown, (Prince Edward Island) and Pictou, N.S.

LOCAL AGENTS:

H. H. KILLEY, Boston,   GEORGE HAYES, Eastport,
C. C. EATON, Portland,   THOMAS JOHNSON, Calais,   B. ANSLEY, St. John.

Tourists will find a trip to the famous "Salmon-Trout" fishing grounds near Calais very desirable, and that to the Lower Provinces for wild scenery and interest in other respects is unsurpassed.

This is the best and cheapest route to all the above places.

PORTLAND AND NEW YORK STEAMSHIP COMP'Y

The new, fast, and splendid Steamships

DIRIGO,

CAPT. H. SHERWOOD,

AND

FRANCONIA,

CAPT. W. W. SHERWOOD,

Will until further notice run as follows:—

LEAVE BROWN'S WHARF, PORTLAND,

AND

PIER 38 EAST RIVER, NEW YORK,

EVERY WEDNESDAY AND SATURDAY

At 4 P.M.

These Steamships are especially adapted for the Route, and are fitted up with fine accommodations for passengers, making this one of the most speedy, safe, and comfortable routes for travellers between

NEW YORK, MAINE, AND CANADA.

Passage in State Rooms $6—Cabin Passage $5

MEALS EXTRA.

EMERY & FOX, Agents, Portland, Me.

H. B. CROMWELL & CO., 86 West St., New York.

1866.
PEOPLE'S LINE STEAMBOATS

BETWEEN

NEW YORK & ALBANY

THE SPLENDID STEAMBOATS

ST. JOHN

AND

DEAN RICHMOND

WILL LEAVE ALBANY EVERY EVENING

(Sundays excepted)

ON THE ARRIVAL OF TRAINS FROM THE NORTH AND WEST,

AND

NEW YORK EVERY EVENING

(Sundays excepted) at 6 o'clock, from the Steamboat Pier

No. 41 North River, foot of Canal Street,

(South side)

Connecting at Albany with Railroad Trains North, West and East.

1866   **DAILY LINE**   **1866**

FOR

ROCHESTER.

The new and magnificent Steel-plated Upper Cabin Steamer

CORINTHIAN

CHRYSLER, MASTER,

Leaves **COBOURG AND PORT HOPE**

Every Day (Sundays excepted)

FOR CHARLOTTE.

———

Passengers in the United States *via* Rochester connect by Special Trains with this Steamer at Charlotte, arrive at Port Hope and Cobourg after a swift and pleasant ride over Lake Ontario, in time for Special Trains to

LINDSAY AND PETERBORO',

and Express Trains East and West on the Grand Trunk Railway, and also for the Royal Mail Line Through Steamers.

———

Passengers in Canada from all points East, West and North, by Rail or Boat, connect with this Steamer at Port Hope and Cobourg, and arrive at Rochester in time for Express Trains East, West and South.

———

THE TABLE AND BAR SUPPLIED WITH THE VERY BEST.

———

BAGGAGE AT OWNERS' RISK, UNLESS BOOKED AND PAID FOR

———

For further information enquire at the Office on board, or of

A. M. BROWN,
General Agent, KINGSTON, C.W.

www.ingramcontent.com/pod-product-compliance
Lightning Source LLC
Chambersburg PA
CBHW021012240426
43669CB00037B/650